FOOD BECOMES YOU

RUTH M. LEVERTON

RUTH M. LEVERTON, Ph.D., is
Assistant Administrator of
The Agricultural Research Service
U.S. Department of Agriculture

FOOD BECOMES YOU

IOWA STATE UNIVERSITY PRESS-Ames, Iowa

First edition © 1952 by the University of Nebraska Press

Second edition, 1960

Second printing, 1961
Third printing, 1961
Fourth printing, 1962

Third edition, 1965

Second printing, 1966
Third printing, 1969
Fourth printing, 1973

Library of Congress Catalog Card Number: 65–19382

To each of "YOU"

in

Food Becomes YOU

Acknowledgments

Food Becomes YOU is a kind of hybrid. Its information comes from research. Its philosophy comes from the evidence and knowledge that food is a strong force in every person's life. Its style is the result of years of experience in explaining food and nutrition facts to mothers, fathers, youngsters, oldsters, and in-betweeners, collectively and individually.

It is a pleasure to express appreciation for the helpfulness of many friends and colleagues, especially those who used the first and second editions and encouraged me to prepare this revision, and for the valuable suggestions given by interested staff members of the Agricultural Research Service, U.S. Department of Agriculture, the Nutrition Section of the Children's Bureau, U.S. Department of Health, Education and Welfare, and the Iowa State University Press.

Grateful acknowledgment is made for the use of "A Daily Food Guide" and the "Table of Food Values" developed and published by the Agricultural Research Service, U.S.D.A.; material from my booklet "A Girl and Her Figure" published by the National Dairy Council, Chicago, Illinois; and the "Physical Growth Records" prepared by the Joint Committee on Health Problems in Education of the National Education Association and the American Medical Association.

Ruth M. Leverton

Washington, D.C.
February, 1965

Table of Contents

List of Tables

Little Miss T.

It's a very odd thing —
As odd as can be —
That whatever Miss T. eats
Turns into Miss T;
Porridge and apples,
Mince, muffins and mutton,
Jam, junket, jumbles —
Not a rap, not a button
It matters; the moment
They're out of her plate,
Though shared by Miss Butcher
And sour Mr. Bate;
Tiny and cheerful,
And as neat as can be,
Whatever Miss T. eats
Turns into Miss T.

—Walter de la Mare

Quoted by permission

1.

Food's the Thing

Everything in your body was once in your food.

Starting with a single cell, growing to your present size, and for as long as you live — food becomes YOU.

Food becomes your blood and bones, your brain and brawn.

Food becomes your size and strength, your energy and stamina.

Food contributes to your personality, effectiveness, and emotional stability.

Moreover, food is becoming to you — the right kind and amount, that is — because it gives you the appearance and feeling of radiant health. This is the result of good nutrition.

Food is part of your nutrition. Nutrition includes everything that happens to food — from the time you eat it until it is used for building, repairing, and operating the body. Nutrition is the result of the kind of food supplied and the body's use of that food.

If your nutrition is poor, you are seriously handicapped. You tire easily, you lack stamina, purpose, and enthusiasm. You are a drudge and a drag; you are subject to discontent, worry, and irritability. Poor nutrition is an insidious thing. Sometimes it creeps into your life, like a spy, and slyly sabotages your enjoyment. Other times it attacks outright and quickly defeats everything you try to do.

Your nutrition can be an asset or a handicap to you depending on whether it is good or poor. You are the person who has the most to do about your nutrition and the food that becomes you.

Scientists are working constantly to increase our knowledge about food and nutrition and to find ways of applying this knowledge to the benefit of individuals and of nations. Whether you benefit from this knowledge depends on whether you use it in choosing the foods your body needs to be well nourished.

Perhaps you are thinking that you do not know how to do this. You don't have to be a nutritionist or a food scientist to select wisely the food that becomes you.

If you have a dependable source of information and follow intelligently the directions given, you can choose food for health and vigor.

The chapters ahead are your source of information — a handbook to guide you in selecting the food that becomes you. Follow it confidently and be not only well fed, but also be well nourished.

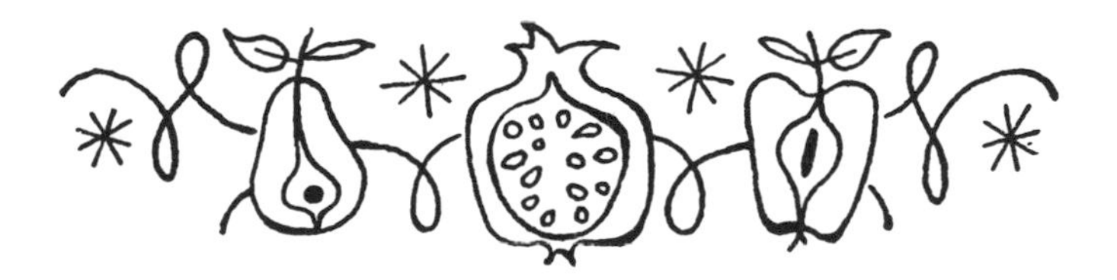

2.

Food Habits

HABIT IS A POWERFUL FORCE in determining the food that becomes us. We eat according to our established food habits — and like all habits these can be good or they can be poor.

Food habits are the sum of our attitudes and ideas, our likes and dislikes, and our experience and practices of choosing and eating food.

Our food habits are good when we are willing to eat the kinds and amounts of food which science has proved we need for optimum nutrition. Good food habits mean that we know food becomes us, that we mean to supply the best and become the best. "Willingness to eat" does not mean that we have to like all kinds of food equally well. Most of us have special preferences, favorite foods, and also definite dislikes. A willingness to eat means a promise to ourselves that we will not confine our food selections to favorite foods, especially when doing so leads to poor diet and on to nutritional bankruptcy.

Poor food habits mean that we eat only what we like regardless of what we need, and that we have a closed-door policy toward change. Often we do not realize that our food habits may be built on whim and prejudice and indifference. When we become aware of this we have taken the first step toward building better food habits.

FOOD AND FIRST IMPRESSIONS

Food habits begin to form with our earliest experience with food. As babies we had our first experience with people through food, and from this we got our first impressions about the world in general. If we had food when we wanted and needed it, then we got the idea that people were nice and friendly and comforting and that the world was rosy. But if we had to cry until we were exhausted each time before we were fed, we got different impressions. We thought the world was a tough place, where we had to fight even for our food. Certainly we did not have a comfortable, happy association between people and food.

The present trend in infant feeding is to permit a baby to set his own feeding schedule according to *his* hunger instead of *our* clock. This makes him more satisfied and comfortable; he gains the impression that food is wonderful and the world is a nice place with nice people in it.

Perhaps as children we were greatly confused about the place of food in our world. Even though it was a basic need like shelter and clothing, food was used in many ways that had nothing to do with our need for it. Sometimes we had to eat things that mother said tasted "good-good" and yet nobody else ate. Other times we were not given things because mother said they tasted "bad-bad" and yet we saw the grownups having second servings. Soon we learned to use food as a weapon to fight back at the world and at parental authority in particular.

Sometimes our parents used food to discipline us, giving us extra or special kinds as a reward, or sending us to bed without any to punish us. A child soon learns he can please or displease his parents, gain attention or create a crisis by eating or not eating — depending on what he wants to accomplish.

Poor food habits often develop because we use food in ways that it is not meant to be used. Basically food is for life and health and security, not for punishment and reward and attention-getting.

ATTITUDES AND ACTIONS

Why are we so concerned with the food habits that children are forming? First, because at every age the body must be supplied with the right materials in sufficient amounts if it is to grow and develop to the full extent of its possibilities. This is especially true the first twenty years of life. Food must provide our chief source of these materials.

Second, the eating habits and attitudes we form as children dictate much of what we eat when we are adults. We grow up eating certain foods prepared in certain ways, and as adults we almost unconsciously expect and prefer to eat in the same way. If we do not have the foods we are accustomed to, we often try to change things — where we eat, how the food is prepared, or who prepares it.

One of our responsibilities as parents is to equip our children with good habits in every phase of living. Good food habits at any age do not just happen. Without guidance a child may form the habit of eating too much food, of eating too little food, or of not eating some of the nutritionally important foods. The terms *self-selection, self-direction,* or *self-demand,* as used in child feeding, are not meant to imply self-indulgence or self-destruction of health by poor food habits.

A child learns by example and experience what to eat and what to think about food. It is not uncommon for parents to give their children the best possible social and educational advantages and yet deny them a most important ingredient of good health by setting a poor example of what to eat and what to think about food.

Example also may influence a child's attitude toward new food experiences. When he visits a place near the seacoast will he want to try the flavor of fish unknown to him in the Midwest? Or will he resist the new taste adventure and order what he is used to so he can stay in his own little food world? A person's interest in new foods and flavors is usually one indication of the breadth of his social experience and his interest in the world beyond his own back yard.

FOOD AND ASSOCIATIONS

We think of certain foods in connection with certain experiences or situations, and these associations account for some of our food habits. We may think of soft, milky foods in connection with illness and therefore consider them unsuitable for well folks; we may associate salads with feminine luncheons and think of salads as "sissy foods" for men; we may feel that because puddings are eaten with a spoon instead of a fork they are "childish" food. Those raised on a farm may believe skim milk is fit only for pigs. Some of us think that organ meats such as liver, heart, and kidney are inferior or "not nice."

We have special associations with the foods we ourselves ate on busy, steamy wash-days, the foods we had when company came, the foods we ate when we were away from home, at grandmother's house, at church suppers, and at Fourth of July picnics. Sunday foods and holiday foods were an important and usually happy part of our childhood experiences.

It is not uncommon for our war veterans or people from war-torn countries to have an extreme revulsion for the kind of food they were given during times of stress, even though the food may have saved their lives. Sometimes long afterwards, through association alone, they become ill just from the sight or smell of it.

We rate some foods as "high class" because they are of superior quality or size, or are unusual, or simply because they are expensive and suggest social standing. On the other hand we are likely to rate foods that are used by people on relief or are included in low-cost meals as "low class" because they suggest charity and poverty to us.

A LITTLE CHECKUP

Appetite alone is not a reliable guide to what we need to eat for wise weight and good nutrition. Many foods are high in appetite appeal and low in nutritive value. Therefore, it is wise to check up on our food habits occasionally. The kinds and amounts of foods we need for good nutrition will be discussed in the chapters ahead. We should check to see if we and others in our family are eating these regularly.

Appetite is our *desire* for food, hunger is our *need* for it. Few of us ever feel the pain that goes with real hunger, because our habit of eating several times a day renews our energy supply before hunger broadcasts any urgent distress signals.

How we look and feel tells us something about our food habits. At every age the outward and visible signs of good nutrition are usually apparent in our physical appearance, our disposition, our emotional reactions, and our vigor and stamina.

It is safer and easier to build good food habits than to correct poor ones. But ridding ourselves of poor food habits need not be hard if we stop trying to find excuses for them. Sometimes it helps to look into the reasons for them. Often we find we do not know these reasons;

we have forgotten the unpleasant associations which are responsible for our dislike of certain foods. We then can start to build pleasant associations with these foods, or at least we can arrive at a neutral "enlightened" attitude and eat them when we know we need them. Often unpleasant food associations and habits of omissions can be unveiled for what they are — barriers to good nutrition.

Improving our food habits can be an adventure in eating many kinds of good food. The first step is to recognize that we can profit by bringing our ideas and actions about food and eating up-to-date. The second is to get sensible, accurate information about food and health, and the third step is to use this information in choosing the food that becomes us. We'll find it can be fun and definitely rewarding.

3.

Wise Weight

SOMETHING THAT INTERESTS almost everyone is weight — the problem of taking it off, putting it on, or just keeping it normal. Weight is one of the most talked-about subjects, and rightly so, for it can affect our vitality, our appearance, our personal and public relations, our emotional adjustments, and our length of life.

Weight alone does not tell the whole story of our health, but it comprises a very important chapter. Many of us who are overweight or underweight insist that we are perfectly healthy. But probably we would be much surprised to find out how much better we would feel if our weight were normal.

WHAT IS NORMAL WEIGHT?

The normal or desirable weight for each of us depends on our age, height, and body build.

Usually body weight continues to increase during the late teens and through the twenties. Although we stop growing in height some time between our fifteenth and twentieth birthdays, the body goes on building in other ways. On a good diet the body deposits minerals inside the bones to make them stronger. It puts protein into the muscles and the vital working organs to make firm, sturdy tissues. It tucks some fat here and there for shock absorbers, insulation, and pleasing curves. Finally it builds up a nutritional savings account for use in emergencies. By the time we are 25 or 30 years old, this growing process is over and so is our need for adding weight.

Our weight should not increase after we reach the age of 25 or 30. When we are 40 we have no reason to weigh more than when we were 30, nor when we are 60 to weigh more than when we were 50. In spite of this, a great many men and women gain about a pound a year after age 30 or 40. A pound a year may seem too little even to mention. By the end of 15 or 20 years, however, that many extra pounds certainly are not too little to notice!

Height is important in determining our normal weight. The taller we are, the more we must weigh to be well proportioned and well nourished. Each added inch of height means longer and heavier bones, larger muscles, more blood and blood vessels, and slightly larger vital working parts.

BODY BUILD

Body build refers to the size and width of our bone structure in relation to our height. This proportion affects what we should weigh. The larger our build, the more we need to weigh to look and be well. Narrow shoulders and hips and small wrists mean a small build. People of this build are often shorter than average. Wide shoulders and hips and large wrists indicate a large build, and people with such a build are often taller than average. Most of us have a medium or average build, neither extra small nor large.

We can judge our own build by comparing the size of our bones with other people who are about the same height. Here's a warning, though: If we are overweight, we are likely to overrate our body build and decide that it is a large build when it is only medium or maybe even small. We may do this quite unconsciously in trying to justify our extra weight. Our bone structure would look much smaller if we could see it without so much padding. If we are underweight, we may underestimate our build and the weight it should carry.

WEIGHTS FOR HEIGHTS

We have little influence over our height and build but we can control how much weight we carry on this

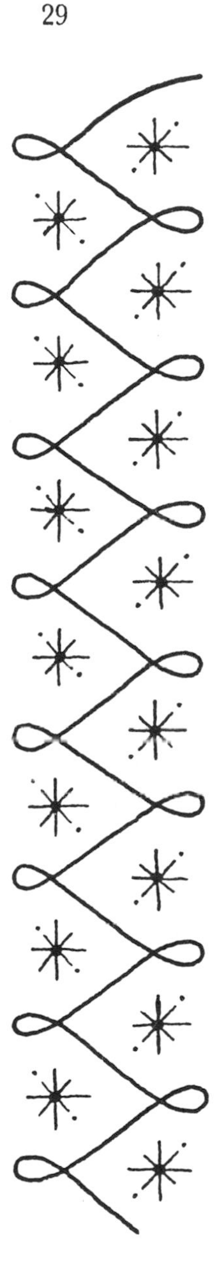

TABLE 1
WEIGHTS FOR HEIGHTS OF MEN AND WOMEN*

Height	*Weights for Men*			*Weights for Women*		
	Low	*Average*	*High*	*Low*	*Average*	*High*
Inches	*Pounds*	*Pounds*	*Pounds*	*Pounds*	*Pounds*	*Pounds*
60	—	—	—	100	109	118
61	—	—	—	104	112	121
62	—	—	—	107	115	125
63	118	129	141	110	118	128
64	122	133	145	113	122	132
65	126	137	149	116	125	135
66	130	142	155	120	129	139
67	134	147	161	123	132	142
68	139	151	166	126	136	146
69	143	155	170	130	140	151
70	147	159	174	133	144	156
71	150	163	178	137	148	161
72	154	167	183	141	152	166
73	158	171	188	—	—	—
74	162	175	192	—	—	—
75	165	178	195	—	—	—

Measurements made without shoes and other clothing.

From "Trends in Heights and Weights," Milicent L. Hathaway, *1959 Yearbook of Agriculture, FOOD,* U.S. Government Printing Office, Washington 25, D.C.

*If you have a small build, use the low figure. If you have a large build, use the high figure. The figure for the average will be suitable for most.

body structure. Table 1 is a guide to desirable weights for men and women of different heights. The weights are based on part of a nationwide study made by the American College Health Association in 1948–50 of about 160,000 college students — men from 25 to 29 years old, and women from 20 to 24 years old. The low and high figures in the table refer to the range in weights found among persons of the same height. The weights are a little lower for the women than the ones given in most of the former height-weight tables. Adults between 20 and 30 years old have become taller than adults of the same age were in the 1900 to 1930 period, and the women weigh a little less for their height than they did then. Children are both taller and heavier at every age than they were in the early 1900's.

In adapting this table, which applies to all of us, for specific application to yourself, consider your build. If you have a small build, the low figure would be more likely to be desirable for you than the average or high figures. If you have a large build, use the high figure as your guide. The figure for the average will be suitable for most of us.

A range of 3 pounds below to 3 pounds above the figures given in the table is permissible for weights under 140 pounds, and 5 pounds above or below for weights over 140 pounds. Don't abuse this leeway by stretching it!

WEIGHING IN

Remember two things when you weigh yourself.

First, weigh at the same time of day and, if possible, on the same scale each time. Your weight may vary as much as 2 or 3 pounds during a single day, depending on your water intake and loss and on the number of hours since the last meal. If you have a scale at home, the best time to weigh is when you first get up in the morning and before you dress or eat. If you use scales away from home, try to use the same one each time you weigh. Not all scales weigh the same, especially the ones with springs. Try to wear about the same kind of clothing — especially shoes — each time. Wearing shorts one time and a heavy suit the next or sport shoes one time and light pumps the next will surely confuse your weight record. If you are checking closely on your weight, it is wise to weigh under the same conditions every other day for a week and use the average of these weights as a starting point for gaining or losing.

Second, compare your weight with the desirable weight for your height and build, as well as with how much you weighed last time. Suppose you weigh 140 pounds today and you say, "That's just a pound more than last week. A pound doesn't mean anything because my weight varies more than that in a single day." But wait! Did you say the same thing last week and the weeks before that? You should be saying, "I weigh 5 pounds more than my normal weight. Last week it was only 4 pounds and the week before only 3 pounds. I'd better stop gaining!" Unless you compare your weight with what it should be, you may edge pound by pound toward overweight and the problems it brings. If you are underweight, you could become more so if you compare your weight only with what it was last week or last month instead of with what it should be.

SUPPLY AND DEMAND

What determines our weight? We know it's more than just the food we eat. For comparison let's ask, "What determines our bank balance?" We know it's not just the size of our pay check. No, it's the balance between what we earn and what we spend — our supply and our demand — that determines whether we have money left over, whether we just come out even, or whether we have to draw on our savings. Our weight is the balance between the energy supplied by the food we eat and the energy we spend for every minute of being alive. What determines our demand for energy and how food energy supplies this demand are explained in the next two chapters.

4.

Activity and Calories

Food energy provides the power the body needs for all its activities: to move, to breathe, to keep the heart beating, to keep warm, and to help in growth and upkeep. Supplying energy is one of the chief jobs of the food we eat. First the food is digested and then it is taken by the blood stream to the cells in all parts of the body. The blood stream also picks up oxygen from the lungs and takes it to the cells. The food combines with the oxygen — we say it is "oxidized" — and energy is released for our needs. Foods are storehouses of energy. Food cannot supply energy as it waits in the cupboard or refrigerator, but when it is eaten, digested, and then oxidized the stored energy is released for the body's use.

TO MEASURE ENERGY

We measure energy in *calories* just as we measure height in inches or weight in pounds. The energy stored in food is measured in calories and so is the energy we use for all our body activities. Sometimes it is said that we "eat calories." Actually we eat foods that yield energy and the energy is measured in calories.

When we eat the amount of food that supplies the same number of calories as we need to meet our energy demands, our weight does not change.

When we eat more food than we need to meet our energy demands, the excess is stored in the body as fat, and we *gain* weight.

When we eat too little food to meet our energy demands, body fat is oxidized to release energy to make up the shortage, and we *lose* weight.

One pound of fat has the energy value of about 3,500 Calories.

To gain a pound of fat we have to deposit in our energy account 3,500 Calories more than we need to maintain a constant weight. Then one pound of fat will be added to the body.

To lose a pound of body fat we have to overdraw our energy account by 3,500 Calories. To cover this debt the body will oxidize (burn) some of the fat it has stored in the tissues. It takes one pound of this fat to supply 3,500 Calories. Then the body will have one pound less of fat.

WHAT KIND OF ACTIVITY?

The amount of energy, or the number of calories, we need each day depends on the amount of both the involuntary and the voluntary activity of the body.

Involuntary activity includes the automatic actions of the body, such as the work of the heart, the lungs, and other specialized organs and of keeping the muscles alert so they can act when they receive commands. The calorie need for involuntary activity is an absolute must and has to be met every minute of our lives regardless of other needs. An adult needs about 10 to 12 Calories for each pound of body weight each 24 hours for this purpose, sometimes called *basal metabolic rate.* Usually this amounts to considerably more than the number of calories we need for our voluntary activity. The pace-setter for our involuntary activity is a chemical made by the thyroid gland in the neck. It is a hormone called thyroxin. Occasionally there is too much thyroxin and the pace is too fast, or there is not enough and the pace is too slow. Abnormal basal metabolic rate requires a physician's care and usually can be corrected.

Voluntary activity is what we choose to do, such as using our muscles for walking, bending, running, sitting, writing, and every motion over which we have control. The amount of energy required for voluntary activities depends on the size and number of muscles we use and how long and how strenuously we use them.

It takes more energy to use many muscles than to use just a few. Contrast the number of muscles we use walking and sitting.

It takes more energy to use large muscles than small ones. Contrast the size of the muscles we use swimming and typing.

It takes more energy to move muscles rapidly than to move them slowly. Contrast the speed of moving muscles in running and in walking.

It takes more energy to use muscles a long time than a short time. Contrast the time that leg muscles are used in walking 2 miles and in walking 1 block.

Then, the more energy we use the more calories we need.

Unusual or extreme nervous tension increases our energy need because it increases the contraction and activity of the muscles. Under such tension some people may eat less than usual while others may eat more. Mental work does not increase our energy requirement enough to count. One-half of a salted peanut will supply enough energy for an hour of intense mental effort!

You can estimate your total energy need, or your calorie requirements, on the basis of your level of activity — how much and how fast you move around in your work and play. First decide in which one of these activity groups you belong.

Rate yourself as *sedentary* if most of your time is spent in light muscular activity — a good deal of sitting and standing and moving around in a relatively small space — and if you take your recreation in mild forms with only occasional times of activities such as swimming or square dancing.

The majority of adults, especially women, rate as sedentary. This includes professional and white-collar workers; many blue-collar workers, especially if they work indoors; housewives with small families or with larger families and many labor-saving devices or someone to help with the housework.

Rate yourself as *active* if you use more muscles and move faster and more continuously than the people who are rated as sedentary. A postman, truck driver, gardener, farmer during seasons of light work, janitor, factory worker, waitress, and some housewives who do all of their own housework and also take care of gardens and yards would rate as active.

Do not rate yourself as *very active* unless you are a farmer in the busiest season; a student in strenuous competitive sports such as football, basketball, or track and practicing several hours a day; a heavy construction worker, miner, logger, longshoreman, or a person doing things that require heavy work of many muscles for many hours each day. Few women rate as very active.

When you have rated yourself as sedentary, active, or very active, write down your weight. If you are overweight or underweight, write down the desirable weight for your height and build.

To estimate your total daily energy need multiply your desirable body weight by:

16 Calories if you are sedentary
20 Calories if you are active
24 Calories if you are a very active woman
or 28 Calories if you are a very active man.

> These figures are given as calories per pound of body weight because a large person has more body substance to keep up and move around than a small person and, therefore, needs a few more calories for everything he does — but only a few.

The number of calories in your answer is not a rigid rule; it is only a guide to help you in adjusting your food supply of energy to the energy requirement of your general level of activity. The answer given by this calculation is likely to be a little high for a large person with a desirable weight over 160 pounds, and a little low for a small person with a desirable weight under 120 pounds. Your weight is the test of how well you are balancing your supply and demand for calories.

Try not to overestimate your activity when you are calculating how many calories you need. Most of us think we are much more active than we really are. For example, when we spend a couple of hours at the swimming pool, we think we are being very active. We forget that probably we spend three-fourths of the time sunning ourselves, floating, watching others swim or dive, visiting with friends, and being generally relaxed and inactive.

Middle-aged and older persons require from 5 to 10 per cent fewer calories than in their earlier adult years. Our basal metabolism decreases as we grow older, and usually we become less active. Not many of us, however, reduce the amount of food we eat — our calorie supply — as much as our calorie requirement is reduced. The result is a storage of the extra calories as fat. This situation is so prevalent that many of us mistake a slow accumulation of weight as part of the normal process of aging!

Automation, labor-saving devices, and the use of horsepower instead of human power all keep us from having to use as much energy for everyday living as we used in the past. Contrast the amount of physical work that went into keeping a home and feeding a family twenty, thirty, or fifty years ago with the amount required now.

Even easy tasks are being made easier. New labor-saving devices are coming on the market almost daily. Egg beaters, can openers, ice-cube crushers, pencil sharpeners, and even scissors are being motorized to save us energy.

Adapting ourselves to the modern sedentary and mechanized way of life — without gaining undesirable weight — means one of two things for most of us: either we must increase our voluntary activity, or we will have to be mildly hungry all of the time.

If we rate in the sedentary group we need consciously to organize our lives to include some regular physical activity that uses the larger muscles and keeps them firm and active. Even mild activity can be effective in keeping muscle tone, using calories, and controlling weight.

Walking is one of the simplest and most satisfactory means of exercising. It requires about 1.7 Calories per pound per hour. The distance you cover determines how many calories you spend more than does the speed at which you walk.

Walking a mile requires about 70 Calories for a person who weighs 120 pounds, about 90 Calories for one who weighs 160 pounds, or 105 Calories for one who weighs 180 pounds.

Of course, you do not always walk an entire mile at one time, but whatever distance you cover, the exercise will use a proportional number of calories.

A 160-pound man would spend about 180 Calories if he walked 2 miles to his office. But if he drove his car and spent the time thus saved working at his desk or reading the paper, he would spend only about 85 Calories — a difference of 95 Calories! For a 120 pound person the difference would be about 70 Calories.

A typist who weighs 120 pounds uses 15 Calories an hour *less* if her typewriter is an electric one than if it is a standard machine. Perhaps 15 Calories seem like too few to take seriously. But if she uses an electric typewriter instead of a standard one for 5 hours a day, she could save enough energy in a working year of 50 weeks to gain 5½ pounds! The only way she can keep from gaining weight is to eat less or exercise more to compensate for the energy she saves by using the electric typewriter.

Exercise gives us many benefits in addition to using energy and helping to control weight. It increases blood circulation and muscle tone; it helps to lessen states of tension and fatigue, and to reduce violent emotions; it takes away the vague aches and pains caused by lack of muscular strength and flexibility; and it can add greatly to our enjoyment of work and leisure.

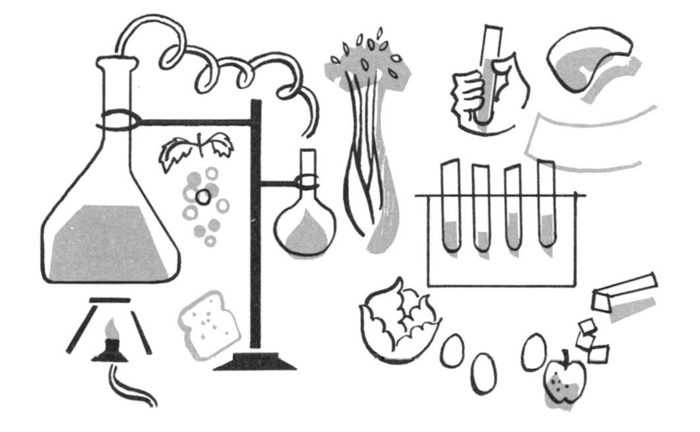

5.

Food and Calories

WE NEED ENERGY for everything we do, but only three kinds of substances in food can supply us with it. Their chemical names are *proteins, carbohydrates* (commonly known as starches and sugars), and *fats.* Each one has a different and complex chemical nature and they all contain the elements carbon, hydrogen, and oxygen. Proteins contain nitrogen, too, which gives them special importance in the body.

The energy values — the number of calories — these substances will give when oxidized in the body are:

Proteins: 115 Calories per ounce or 4 Calories per gram

Carbohydrates: 115 Calories per ounce or 4 Calories per gram

Fats: 255 Calories per ounce or 9 Calories per gram

This is 2¼ times more than the calories from the same amount of proteins or carbohydrates.

The number of calories in a food depends on how much protein, fat, and carbohydrate it contains. If large amounts of these energy-giving substances are present, the food is *high* in calories; if only small amounts are present it is *low* in calories.

Some low calorie foods — such as most fruits and the bulky vegetables — have a large amount of water and fiber; these substances are valuable to the body but do not supply energy. Other low calorie foods such as skim milk have lots of water and little or no fat. High calorie foods contain a large proportion of the energy-givers and relatively little water and fiber. Compare a piece of frosted cake with a bowl of tossed vegetable salad. The cake contains protein, fat, and carbohydrate from the combination of eggs, milk, sugar, shortening, and flour. These may add up to as much as 300 or 400 Calories. The salad, on the other hand, contains foods high in water and fiber with only a small amount of carbohydrate. It supplies about 25 Calories. If you add oil or mayonnaise to the salad you can add calories rapidly (each tablespoonful will add 100 Calories) because fats are concentrated sources of energy.

HOW MANY CALORIES?

The most practical thing for us to know about calories is how many there are in the servings of food we usually eat. Most of us know pretty well what quantities to visualize when we think of servings of common foods. Some foods, such as apples and many other fruits, have a natural serving size — one is a serving. Some servings can be described in kitchen measures, such as teaspoons, tablespoons, cups, and fractions of a recipe. Other servings can be described in units such as slices of bread (if you buy it sliced), fractions of a head of lettuce, and the number of servings in a pound of meat.

The calorie value of servings of our most common foods are given in the Table of Food Values beginning on page 171. Foods similar in composition are grouped together. We always associate foods such as meat, fish, and poultry with each other whether we are planning a meal, hunting them in the food market, or learning their nutritive values. The same is true of fruits and vegetables, dairy products, breads and cereals, fats and sugars.

A QUICKIE

Sometimes a general guide to calorie values is helpful if we want to know whether a food is high or low in calories rather than exactly how many calories it has. We can get a hint of calorie value from the characteristics of flavor and texture that sugar, fat, fiber or roughage, and water give to foods. Try this as a guide:

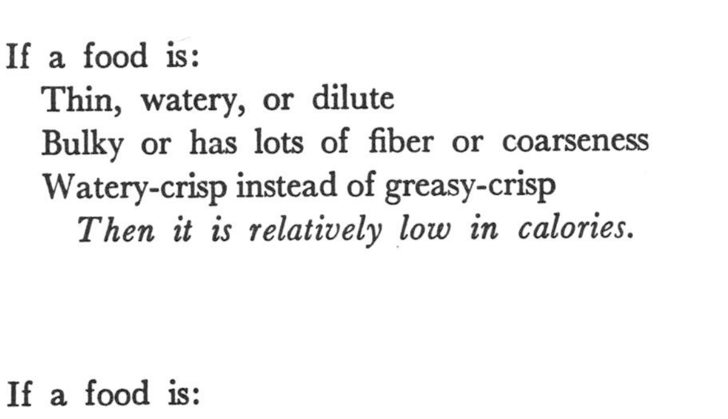

If a food is:
Thin, watery, or dilute
Bulky or has lots of fiber or coarseness
Watery-crisp instead of greasy-crisp
Then it is relatively low in calories.

If a food is:
Thick, oily, or greasy-crisp
Slick, smooth, or gooey
Sweet or sticky
Compact or concentrated
Alcoholic
Then it is relatively high in calories.

Now you can compare a chocolate malt with a glass of skim milk or orange juice, or an avocado salad with a tossed green salad.

LONE-WOLF CALORIES

Calories are often referred to as "keeping company" with the other nutrients present in foods. "Choose your calories by the company they keep," is good advice. The calories in milk, for example, keep company with protein, calcium, and riboflavin plus other minerals and vitamins. The calories in meat keep company with protein, important B vitamins, and minerals. On the other hand, calories in sugar, some cooking fats, and some unenriched refined cereals do not keep company with other nutrients. We call these "lone-wolf" calories to describe their lack of nutritive companions. Alcohol, too, has lone-wolf calories.

Eating too many foods with lone-wolf calories is a poor food habit. Either it crowds out the calories which keep company with essential nutrients or it increases our calorie supply above our requirement and leads to overweight.

Even though they are flavorful and enjoyable, lone-wolf calories must not dominate what we eat. We can welcome such calories into our diet after we have supplied our other nutritive needs and *until,* but not after, we have supplied our calorie requirement.

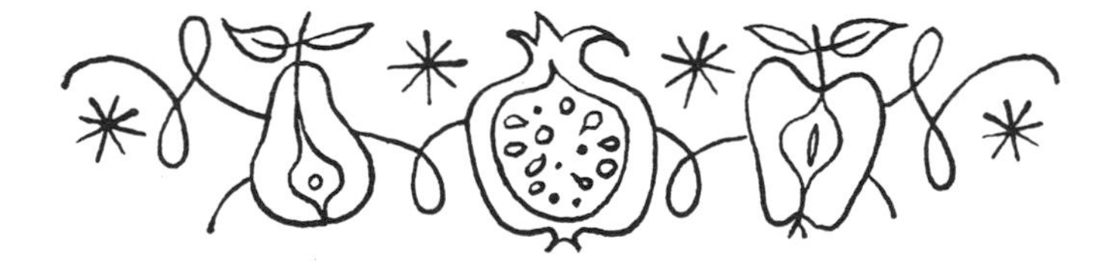

6.

Trimming That Figure

IF WHENEVER WEIGHT IS MENTIONED your first reaction is "I wish I weighed less" or "I really should reduce," this chapter is for you. No one really wants to be overweight.

If you are a person who weighs too much, whether a little or a lot, you might recall all of the arguments you have heard against people being overweight. Excess weight is inconvenient; it can spoil your looks, threaten your vanity, and put you on the defensive about life in general. Also, it can be a health hazard. Compared with people of normal weight, those who are overweight are more likely to have gall bladder trouble, diabetes, gout, and arthritis; they are poor surgical risks and less resistant to infections. They are more likely to have hardening of the arteries and high blood pressure than lean people. Overweight also places an extra burden on the heart. Those are but a few of the involvements.

But instead of these arguments, think of what you can *become* weight-wise and figure-wise and health-wise. Visualize yourself as you want to be and then work and eat with that goal in mind. Equip yourself with these essentials:

1. Your doctor's approval of your reducing.
2. A scientifically sound food plan with menus to keep you healthy though losing weight.
3. Enough information to give you the reasons for what you are doing.

Add to these a good supply of patience, will power, and determination for the first two or three weeks. After that the reward of losing weight will help to keep you happily on your diet. Now plan to enjoy the experience and to glory in your own achievement.

There are many false ideas about being overweight. You have heard them often — perhaps you have even used them as alibis for your own plumpness. Let's look at the facts.

Fallacy: "I come from a fat family; therefore I guess I was meant to be fat."

Fact: **Overeating is often a family habit — and then the whole family is overweight. Our calorie supply depends on our eating habits, and the**

habit of overeating brings overweight. When you eat with a family in which everyone is overweight, you usually have foods cooked in extra fat and cream to add flavor, have second and third helpings because things are so good, have rich and sweet desserts, and have bedtime snacks that by themselves would supply a good share of the day's calorie need.

Fallacy: Overweight people need less food energy than normal people do because their metabolism is low. "Everything I eat goes to fat because my metabolism is low."

Fact: **Most overweight people have normal metabolic rates. Their overweight does not come from a subnormal calorie need. (When it is subnormal it can be treated by the doctor.) Actually they need more energy to do a piece of work than do people of normal weight. It takes more calories to support overweight people, and to move them around, to take them upstairs or to move any part of them. Just ask yourself which is less work, moving a straight chair or an overstuffed one.**

Fallacy: Overweight people use their food more economically than normal people do. "I get more from my food than you do from yours."

Fact: **Overweight people get more food energy because they eat more food. Just follow them around for a day or sit beside them at a meal. They don't think they eat anything much, but they are likely to eat the extra roll and butter that someone doesn't want, and they use the extra cream left by someone who drinks his black.**

The reasons for overeating and being overweight often can be found in the answers to some searching questions. When you decide to reduce, have a private talk with yourself and get honest answers to these personal questions:

What and how much do I eat?

For three days keep a list of everything you eat and how much. It may enlighten you as much as it has enlarged you. You may find you are eating a little more or a lot more of everything than you realized. If you don't feel well when you try to eat less, it is probably because you choose too many lone-wolf calories and skimp on the calories that keep good company with vitamins, minerals, and protein.

When do I eat?

You may be eating between meals more often than you think you do, and then you may be skipping meals to try to counteract your constant snacking. Eating so often and eating irregularly may be a sign you are tired, worried, lonesome, dissatisfied, or just restless and disorganized. You may not be wearing your heart on your sleeve but you may be wearing your frustrations on your frame.

Why do I eat more than I need?

Every time you start to eat something ask yourself, "Why am I eating this?" You'll be surprised at some of your answers, especially if they are honest ones. They may be something like these: "I'm eating to put off doing something I don't want to do." "Something disagreeable has happened and eating will help me forget it." "Something wonderful has happened and I'm eating to celebrate." "I'm discouraged, and eating makes me feel better." "Everyone but me is having fun at the dance so I'm trying to drown my sorrows in this extra thick malt."

What satisfactions do I get from being overweight? Do you think you've been happier since you've been overweight? Maybe so, but what was happening at the same time that you were gaining weight?

Perhaps you started to gain soon after you were married because you were happy and not working as hard as you had been before. Then, as your family and responsibilities grew, you worked harder and thought you needed extra food, so you ate more.

Maybe you started to gain weight after your children grew up or after you moved to a streamlined apartment. You had more time for bridge and snacks, or golf and lunch. All these are the sources of your happiness; overweight just followed along.

Perhaps you began to gain weight after you landed the job you had always dreamed of. Then came more prestige and security, more money, and more of the right contacts in your business and social life.

All these are the things that made you happier rather than the excess weight you added to your frame as you went along.

Losing weight can seem like a very slow process. You can't see a change in your weight each time you say "no" to a piece of cake or feel a little hungry and righteous because you ate less than usual for lunch. Sometimes you have to keep on saying *no* and being a little hungry for two or three weeks before the scales will register any less.

When you begin to eat fewer calories than you need, the body exchanges fat for water. When body fat is called into service to supply energy, water temporarily fills the space in the tissues vacated by the fat. The water weighs as much as the fat did, so there is no immediate change in body weight. But the water is not there to stay, and it will leave eventually. You may have to be on a low calorie diet for two or three weeks before the body begins to discard this excess water through the kidneys. As soon as this happens, you begin to weigh less. Your weight may go down quite fast for a few days; then you'll feel gloriously happy and proud that you had the will power to stay with your diet. Then there may be another stretch with no weight change and this will be followed by another drop. This stair-step pattern will be repeated over and over as you get down to the weight you want to be. You must understand what is happening and know what to expect during the time between steps.

Here is what happened to one Mrs. Homemaker when she started to reduce. She followed a low calorie diet faithfully for a month. The diet supplied all of her nutritional needs except that it fell 500 Calories a day short of meeting her energy needs. Because she had to make up this calorie deficit every day by using body fat, she could expect to lose about a pound a week, or between 4 and 5 pounds in a month.

The first week she gained a pound. She was discouraged! The second week she lost a pound. At least she was back where she had started from — but half the month was gone! The third week she neither gained nor lost. She was nearly desperate! In the fourth week she lost 4½ pounds, or the calculated loss for the entire month. Now she thought reducing was wonderful!

These $4\frac{1}{2}$ pounds would never have disappeared if she had given up her diet after two or three weeks because she was discouraged.

It takes a lot of patience and will power to stay on a diet during the discouraging time when the scales don't budge, even though you know you have overdrawn your calorie account and have withdrawn body fat to use for energy.

Are you deciding, "I think I can reduce now that I understand better about calories and food and weight, and about what and why I eat?" Then take these predieting steps.

First, talk to your doctor about your weight problem. Besides needing his approval from a medical standpoint, you will find his interest and moral support most encouraging.

Second, set a reasonable weight as your goal to reach within a certain time. Be realistic about how much you can lose safely and sensibly but still set a goal that will be worthy of your best efforts. Most overweight people can plan to lose $1\frac{1}{2}$ pounds a week safely.

How fast you lose weight will depend on the calorie deficit you create between your supply and your demand for energy. You *must* overdraw your calorie account — spend more for your daily activities than you supply in the food you eat. To meet the deficit the body will use its stored fat. A deficit of 3,500 Calories between supply and demand means the use of one pound of stored fat.

Find your total daily calorie demand for your usual level of activity by multiplying your desirable weight by 16 Calories per pound if you are sedentary or by 20 Calories if you are active (see pages 36 and 37). Then decide how many calories *less* than your need you will supply in the food you eat. How much of a deficit will you choose to live with in order to take some of your unwanted fat out of storage, use it up for energy, and lose weight?

Here is a general guide and timetable for losing 5 pounds of stored fat:

Daily calorie deficit between your supply and demand	*Approximate time required to lose 5 pounds*
300 Calories	60 days
400 Calories	45 days
500 Calories	35 days
600 Calories	30 days
700 Calories	25 days
800 Calories	22 days
900 Calories	20 days
1,000 Calories	18 days

Under ordinary circumstances you can safely plan for a deficit of 500 to 800 Calories a day. If you are a small person, this may be too much, or if you are a large person, you may want to plan for a slightly larger deficit. It is not wise to cut your daily supply of food energy more than 1,000 Calories below your daily need.

Suppose the desirable weight for your height and build is 135 pounds and that your level of activity puts you in the sedentary group. At 16 Calories per pound your total daily energy need would be 2,160 Calories. If you decide on a 500 Calorie deficit for reducing, you would plan to supply 2,160 minus 500, or 1,660 Calories from the food you eat.

You may want to plan to have part of your calorie deficit come from increasing your activity. Walking a mile in addition to your usual activity would increase your need about 85 Calories if you weigh 145 pounds. Then you could count your deficit as 600 Calories.

Whatever the size of your calorie deficit, your success in staying on a reducing diet will depend in a large measure on the nutritional quality of the food you eat. How you feel influences your enthusiasm, your determination and self control, and your disposition.

LOW CALORIE DIETS

There are many ways to plan a diet that is low enough in calories to make your body burn some of its own fat for energy and high enough in nutritive value to keep you in good health. Some scientifically planned and tested low calorie diets emphasize foods rich in protein, others emphasize a generous amount of fat, but never to the exclusion of other important foods. The diet given in this chapter places more emphasis on protein and carbohydrate and less on fat. Personal preference or convenience, or even finances, often affect the kind of low calorie diet chosen for reducing weight.

A reducing diet is given here in two sizes — 1,200 Calories and 1,600 Calories. It was developed and tested under controlled experimental conditions in the nutrition research laboratories of the University of Nebraska. First it was tested on a group of college students. Then it was tested on a variety of overweight people. The menus were adapted for people living and eating in many different kinds of situations: eating at home alone, eating a packed lunch, cooking for and eating with a big family, and eating in restaurants all the time. The diet has proved thoroughly usable, easy to stay on, and therefore successful in taking off weight.

It is called the "Common-Sense Reducing Diet" because this is the secret of its success — common sense in using the best scientific information about food, weight, and energy in our lives, and common sense in following it carefully. The name of the diet may not be glamorous, but the results will be.

This 7-day diet supplies everything the adult body needs in generous amounts to safeguard health. It is low enough in calories to force the body to use stored fat for some of its energy needs. At the same time it is high enough in calories for the body to function normally. It includes a good variety of foods distributed in three meals a day.

The meals are ordinary enough to be the foundation menu for the entire family, making additions of other foods or larger servings for the members who need more food. The lunches are planned for people who are away from home at noon and need to carry a lunch or eat at a restaurant. The same foods that are used in a sandwich could be eaten at home as salad and toast or bread and spread. All the meals could be ordered in even a modest restaurant.

The meals are extremely simple and unadorned. Seasonings, herbs, spices, lemon and lime juice, vinegar, parsley or other green vegetables can be used to add variety in flavor. Adding variety by using dressings, sauces, gravies, toppings, sugar, or nuts is not recommended because these cannot help but add calories.

YOUR COMMON SENSE REDUCING DIET

SUNDAY

	1,200 Calorie Diet	*1,600 Calorie Diet*
Breakfast		
Orange juice	½ cup	same
Egg, boiled or poached	1 medium	same
Bread	1 slice	same
Butter or margarine	½ teaspoon	1 teaspoon
Milk, skim	1 cup	same
Lunch or supper		
Vegetable soup		
Broth, without fat	1 cup	same
Assorted vegetables	¾ cup	same
Crackers	3	6
Cheese or luncheon meat	none	1 ounce
Baked apple	1 small	same
Brown sugar	1 teaspoon	same
Milk, skim	1 cup	same
Dinner		
Baked chicken	3 ounces	same
Riced potatoes	½ cup	¾ cup
Cooked carrots	½ cup	same
Relishes		
Celery	2 stalks	same
Green pepper	3 strips	same
Radishes	3 small	same
Parkerhouse roll	1 small	2 small
Butter or margarine	½ teaspoon	2 teaspoons
Ice cream, plain	¼ pint	same

MONDAY

	1,200 Calorie Diet	*1,600 Calorie Diet*
Breakfast		
Grapefruit	½	same
Oatmeal	½ cup	same
Sugar	1 teaspoon	same
Light cream	none	2 tablespoons
Bread	1 slice	same
Butter or margarine	½ teaspoon	1 teaspoon
Milk, skim	1 cup	same
Lunch or supper		
Cheese sandwich		
Bread	2 slices	3 slices
Butter or margarine	½ teaspoon	2 teaspoons
Processed cheese	1 ounce	1½ ounces
Celery	3 pieces	same
Apple	none	1 medium
Milk, skim	1 cup	same
Dinner		
Baked pork chop, lean	1 chop (⅓ pound raw weight with small bone)	same
Baked potato	½ medium	1 medium
Tossed salad—oil and lemon juice or vinegar dressing	2 teaspoons	same
Lettuce	2 leaves	same
Radishes	3 small	same
Tomato	1 small	same
Bread	1 slice	same
Butter or margarine	1 teaspoon	same
Apricots, fresh or water-pack	3 medium	4 medium

TUESDAY

	1,200 Calorie Diet	*1,600 Calorie Diet*
Breakfast		
Orange	1 medium	same
Egg, boiled or poached	1 medium	same
Bread	1 slice	same
Butter or margarine	½ teaspoon	1 teaspoon
Milk, skim	1 cup	same
Lunch or supper		
Chicken sandwich		
Bread	2 slices	3 slices
Mayonnaise	1 teaspoon	3 teaspoons
Chicken	1 ounce	1½ ounces
Celery	3 pieces	same
Plums, fresh or water-pack	1 medium	2 medium
Milk, skim	1 cup	same
Dinner		
Broiled ground beef, lean	1 serving or ⅕ pound raw weight	same
Mashed potatoes	½ cup	same
Baked squash	⅓ cup	same
Salad in lettuce leaf		
Cabbage	½ cup	same
Apple	½ small	same
Oil dressing	1 teaspoon	same
Parkerhouse roll	1 small	same
Butter or margarine	½ teaspoon	2 teaspoons
Cupcake, plain, unfrosted	none	1 medium

WEDNESDAY

	1,200 Calorie Diet	*1,600 Calorie Diet*
Breakfast		
Grapefruit	½	same
Egg, boiled or poached	1 medium	same
Bread	1 slice	same
Butter or margarine	½ teaspoon	1 teaspoon
Milk, skim	1 cup	same
Lunch or supper		
Tuna fish sandwich		
Bread	2 slices	3 slices
Butter or margarine	½ teaspoon	1 teaspoon
Tuna fish, drained	1 ounce	1½ ounces
Mayonnaise	1 teaspoon	2 teaspoons
Tomato	1 small	same
Apple	none	1 small
Milk, skim	1 cup	same
Dinner		
Creamed dried beef		
Dried beef	2 ounces	same
White sauce*	½ cup	same
Peas	½ cup	same
Relish		
Celery	2 stalks	same
Radishes	4	same
Toast	½ slice	1 slice
Apple pie	1/7 medium pie	same
Ice cream, plain	none	¼ pint

* White sauce: 1 tsp. fat, 1 tsp. flour, ½ cup skim milk.

THURSDAY

	1,200 Calorie Diet	*1,600 Calorie Diet*
Breakfast		
Tomato juice	½ cup	same
Egg, boiled or poached	1 medium	same
Bacon	none	1 strip
Bread	1 slice	same
Butter or margarine	½ teaspoon	1 teaspoon
Milk, skim	1 cup	same
Lunch or supper		
Peanut butter sandwich		
Bread	2 slices	3 slices
Peanut butter	1 tablespoon	2 tablespoons
Green pepper	4 strips	same
Orange	1 small	same
Milk, skim	1 cup	same
Dinner		
Baked ham, lean	2 ounces	same
Mashed sweet potatoes	½ cup	¾ cup
Salad in lettuce leaf		
Apple	½ small	same
Grapes	10 medium	same
Marshmallow	1	same
Oil dressing	1 teaspoon	same
Hard roll	1	same
Butter or margarine	½ teaspoon	1 teaspoon
Oatmeal cookies	2 small	3 small

FRIDAY

	1,200 Calorie Diet	*1,600 Calorie Diet*
Breakfast		
Orange juice	½ cup	same
Ready-to-eat flakes or puffs	½ cup	1 cup
Sugar	1 teaspoon	same
Light cream	none	2 tablespoons
Bread	1 slice	same
Butter or margarine	½ teaspoon	1 teaspoon
Milk, skim	1 cup	same
Lunch or supper		
Egg salad sandwich		
Bread	2 slices	3 slices
Egg, hard cooked	1	2
Mayonnaise	2 teaspoons	3 teaspoons
Dill pickle	¼ pickle	½ pickle
Carrots	3 strips	same
Banana	none	1 small
Milk, skim	1 cup	same
Dinner		
Broiled liver or fish	1 serving, or ⅕ pound raw weight	same
Tartar sauce	1 teaspoon	same
Baked potato	1 medium	same
Green beans	½ cup	same
Tomato	1	same
Hot biscuit	1 small	same
Butter or margarine	1 teaspoon	3 teaspoons
Ice cream, plain	¼ pint	same
Topping	none	1 tablespoon

SATURDAY

	1,200 Calorie Diet	*1,600 Calorie Diet*
Breakfast		
Grapefruit	½	same
Egg, boiled or poached	1 medium	same
Bread	1 slice	same
Butter or margarine	½ teaspoon	1 teaspoon
Jelly	none	1 teaspoon
Milk, skim	1 cup	same
Lunch or supper		
Boiled ham sandwich		
Bread	2 slices	3 slices
Butter or margarine	½ teaspoon	2 teaspoons
Boiled ham, lean	1 ounce	1½ ounces
Gelatin salad		
Cabbage, shredded	½ cup	same
Carrots, grated	¼ cup	same
Green pepper	2 strips	same
Oil dressing	1 teaspoon	same
Milk, skim	1 cup	same
Dinner		
Broiled cube steak	1 serving, or ⅕ pound raw weight	same
French fried potatoes	6 pieces	12 pieces
Head lettuce salad	⅕ head	same
Oil dressing	1 teaspoon	2 teaspoons
Bread	½ slice	1 slice
Butter or margarine	½ teaspoon	1 teaspoon
Angel food cake, unfrosted	1 piece (1/12 of large cake)	same

1. For best results, follow the diet carefully — not in a hit-or-miss fashion. Do not omit any of the foods listed. They are all needed for your good nutrition.

2. Use enriched or whole-wheat breads and cereals.

3. Trim the fat from the meat. Use only the portion that is very lean or streaked with very small lines of fat.

4. Bake or broil the meat to avoid adding fat. If this isn't practical in your case, pan-fry the meat using the least possible amount of fat or oil.

5. Serve vegetables without sauces or added fats.

6. Serve salads with a dressing made of a teaspoon of corn oil or cottonseed oil, plus a little lemon juice or vinegar, and some seasonings.

7. It is permissible to:
   - Use lettuce in the sandwiches.
   - Use tea and coffee without sugar and cream whenever you wish.
   - Use buttermilk in place of skim milk.
   - Change the desserts occasionally as long as you don't add calories.
   - Change a food from one meal to another as long as you eat some breakfast and have some milk, or meat, or egg in every meal.
   - Save a serving of food from one meal to use as a between-meal or a bedtime snack.

8. If you are a teen-ager, a few additions to the reducing diet are necessary to provide enough of the

important foods to meet the nutritional needs of your age group.

To each day's menu *add*
- 2 cups of skim milk *and*
- 1 serving of citrus fruit, or some other good source of vitamin C, *or*
- 1 serving of a vegetable that is a good source of vitamin A, unless the day's menu already includes one.

Consult the Daily Food Guide on pages 96 and 97 to help you make your choices of the fruits and vegetables.

The skim milk will add 180 Calories, and the serving of fruit or vegetable will add from 25 to 100 Calories, depending on what you choose. Look in the Table of Food Values beginning on page 171 to find the calorie value of your different choices.

The 1,600 Calorie diet with these additions is better for most teen-agers than the 1,200 Calorie diet. Only a small, inactive teen-ager would need to use the 1,200 Calorie diet plus, of course, the extra milk and fruit or vegetable.

A few substitutions are permissible but too many are not advisable. Peaches can be used in place of pears, or lettuce can be used in place of cabbage without decreasing the nutritive value of the diet or adding calories. But substituting white potatoes for sweet potatoes on a day when no other deep yellow or green vegetable is served would mean a shortage of vitamin A value. Making substitutions to meet your individual preferences is likely to increase the calories.

If you plan to use a reducing diet with more than 1,200 or 1,600 Calories, consult the Table of Food Values (beginning on page 171) and choose some foods that will add the number of extra calories you want.

If the climb down to your ideal weight is a long one, give yourself a reward at certain "scale" points. Each time you have lost five pounds, you may allow yourself a 500 Calorie bonus and spend it for any foods you want. Perhaps you will want to spend it all for candy, for lone-wolf calories, for larger servings of some of the foods on your diet, or for desserts.

YOU CAN'T DO WITHOUT IT

An indispensable ingredient of any diet is will power and "won't power." It is up to you to decide who is the boss of your reducing plan — you or everybody else. You will get bushels of advice — some of it good and some of it bad, but all of it free. If you can listen with a smile of gracious acceptance and refrain from arguing or giving your views, you are on your way to success. Your confidence will be weakened and your progress hindered if you are susceptible to all of the advice that will be tossed at you, and if you feel you must defend or justify your own plan for reducing. (You will notice that often the advice comes from overweight people who have not used it themselves!)

Do you wonder why some friends so often tease, tempt, and almost force you into breaking your dietary restrictions "just this once" instead of giving you praise or moral support for staying on your diet? They may be urging you to eat, not because they are concerned about you, but because they unconsciously hope that

you will not succeed. When you succeed in losing weight, your overweight friends have a guilty feeling that they should reduce too. They are most comfortable if you fail, because then they can say, "It can't be done so there is no need for me to try it." Someone who is not overweight may think he will lose his feeling of superiority over you if you are no longer overweight.

ADDING CALORIES

When you have arrived at your goal of desirable weight, you can start *slowly* to increase your calorie supply. The first and second week add about 200 Calories a day to the diet you have been using. To supply these additional calories consult the Table of Food Values and choose servings of fruits or vegetables, or meats, or breads and cereals. You can choose different foods each day to give variety to your diet.

The third and fourth week add another 200 Calories a day. Follow the general pattern of the Common-Sense Reducing Diet but begin to make all of your own food choices. Now is the time to test your improved food habits to be sure they are going to keep you fit but trim.

After a week or two of choosing your food and not gaining weight, try adding a few more calories — 100 Calories at a time — until you are eating all of the food you can *without* gaining weight. If at any time your weight begins to creep up, then quickly cut down 100 or 200 Calories or increase your activity to use more calories. It is important to get rid of any added and unwanted weight just as soon as it arrives and not to let it stay around you.

Remember also, if this applies to you, alcohol can be a calorie problem. For some people it may be the chief cause of overweight. The best way to handle the problem is to develop the social art of making one cocktail take the place and the time of three or four. It's also a good idea to beware of the tag-along foods, like canapes, nuts, and dips and chips. The calorie value of alcoholic beverages is given on page 191.

BE HONEST WITH YOURSELF

During this calorie-training period, do some honest bookkeeping. Each day write down what your total calorie need is. Then write down the number of calories in the foods you eat *when you eat them* and add up the calories as you go through the day. This keeps an up-to-the-minute record of how much of your calorie budget you have already spent, and shows you how much you have left to spend. You'll know from this whether you can afford a second homemade roll, or a dish of ice cream, or anything else you like. Honest balancing of your calorie accounts each day will keep you within your budget and save you a lot of mistakes and failures. Getting weighed once a week or oftener will be a check on how well you are doing with your bookkeeping.

You can stop counting every calorie as soon as you have tailored your appetite to keep a normal balance between your supply and demand for energy. You can't wear a size 14 suit if you have a size 20 appetite, nor will a size 10 appetite fit your needs if you are size 16. Appetites have to be tailor-made to fit your individual needs, and nothing is more becoming than a well-fitting appetite. It doesn't bulge or wrinkle in the wrong places, and it does give you style and poise. Part of such a well-tailored appetite is the habit of choosing foods of high nutritive value to supply the many intricate needs of the body for normal functioning and sparkling health.

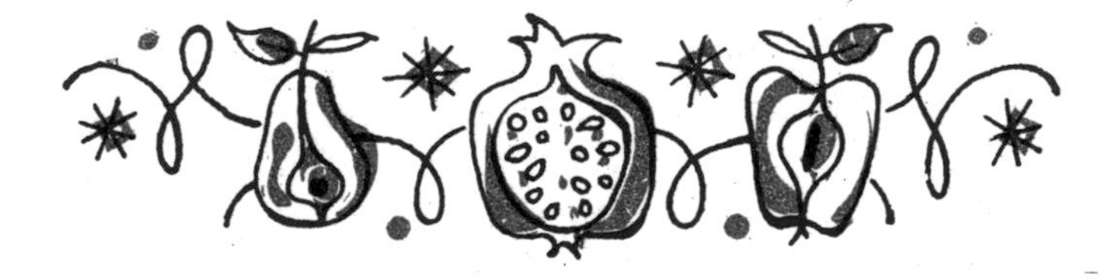

7.

Rounding That Figure

IF YOU WISH your figure had curves in the right places instead of hollows and angles, this chapter is for you. Hollows and angles usually mean underweight, and this can be a handicap to the way you look and feel.

Being underweight can mean lowered resistance, no reserve to use in emergencies, undue fatigue, and poor physical and emotional stamina.

There are many false ideas about being underweight. You have heard them often; perhaps you have even used them to excuse your own thinness. Let's state the facts about some of them.

Fallacy: "I come from a thin family; therefore I guess I was meant to be thin."

Fact: **Our calorie supply depends on our eating habits. The habit of not eating enough to meet our needs results in being underweight. Eating amounts too small may be a family habit; then the whole family will be underweight.**

Fallacy: Underweight people require more energy than do people of normal weight because their metabolism is high. "I can never eat enough to gain weight."

Fact: **Underweight people usually have normal metabolic rates and do not require more food than people of normal weight. Actually they need less energy to do a piece of work because they are light in weight, they require fewer calories to move around, to go up stairs, etc. When the metabolic rate *is* high a physician must be consulted.**

Fallacy: Underweight people are more energetic and ambitious than people of normal weight.

Fact: **The energy and ambition of underweight people usually come from nervousness and are short lived. Such people tire more easily and are likely to have less stamina than people of normal weight. Extreme thinness makes them jumpy, jittery, and tense instead of relaxed and poised.**

The reasons for being underweight can often be found in the answers to certain searching questions. Learning the answers usually makes it easier to start and stay with a plan for gaining. When you decide to gain weight, try having a private talk with yourself to get honest answers to these personal questions:

What and how much do I eat?

Perhaps you are making your body run on half rations. For three days keep a list of everything you eat and how much. Probably it is a little more than usual because keeping a list makes you self-conscious and you try to eat more. Count the calories and compare them with what you need for your activity level and your normal weight. Compare the foods on your list with the Daily Food Guide given in Chapter 9. No doubt you will find several places where you could improve on the quality and quantity of what you eat.

When do I eat?

You may be eating much less than you think you are. You may be skipping meals because you think you aren't hungry or, when you are hungry, eating only very small amounts. On the other hand, you may be eating frequently but the caloric value of the food is not enough to cover your demands. If you eat frequently, you may consciously try to eat less at mealtime, or your appetite may be dulled so that you are not interested in food and so eat very little.

Why don't I eat more?

This is probably a matter of habit. You think you "get full" with very little food. Your stomach is not in the habit of holding as much food as you need because you have let it get out of the practice. Every time you sit down to a meal or to a snack try to eat three more bites than you think you want. These will not make you uncomfortable but will gradually get you in the habit of eating more.

What do I get out of being underweight?

To answer this you must be extremely honest with yourself and try to see behind the front that you present to the world. It is possible that you are getting some kind of special attention because you are underweight. Your friends may worry about you and talk about you a lot — and urge you to eat more. Or they envy you and say, "Oh, if I could only be small like you!" or "I don't see how you eat so little and do so much!" Your thinness may give you a feeling of superiority, especially when you hear your friends fussing about their appetites, their hips, or their waistlines. You may unconsciously wish to stay underweight because you enjoy the satisfaction of being superior to your friends. It is not uncommon for a person to use an underweight condition to express martyrdom to a family or to a job. Such a person wants you to think he is so important to the scheme of things that he cannot waste his precious time or thought on taking care of himself. It is a sort of self-sacrificing attitude calculated to get attention. Needless to say, this person is not showing good judgment or common sense.

Are you among the many men and women who complain that they cannot gain weight or that they actually lose on a high calorie diet? They follow a high calorie diet for a few days or a week and then become discouraged and discard it because they do not gain immediately.

Gaining weight seems like a very slow process to those who are habitually underweight. The body must have 3,500 Calories *in excess* of its need in order to store a pound of fat. To add a pound of fat, therefore, you must eat enough food to supply 3,500 Calories more than the body needs. It may take a week or several weeks to accumulate the calories that will finally make a pound of fat. The scales do not register an increase in your weight each time you eat a hundred extra calories. Sometimes it takes two or three weeks of eating more than your usual amount before your weight starts to climb.

When there are extra calories to be stored as fat, the body discards some of the water in the tissues and stores the fat in its place. This shift causes no change in weight. Eventually the tissue has to absorb water in order to have a normal composition. When this happens, there will be an increase in weight.

You can eat as much as 500 Calories a day more than you need and still stay about the same weight for a week or more. Finally, the newly deposited tissue absorbs water to become normal in composition and then the scales record a sharp gain in weight. Even though a gain may look quite sudden, it comes only as a result of the body having stored fat over a period of several days or weeks.

It is hard to stay on a diet during this discouraging time when the scales do not budge even though you know you have eaten enough food to supply several hundred extra calories.

Just as the best way to save money is not to spend it, so the best way to gain weight is not to spend calories unnecessarily. You must not omit all exercise — some exercise is needed regularly for developing good muscle tone and normal appetite. You should, however, spend some time during the day in resting, preferably lying down, for additional rest is a thrifty way to save some energy. If you can't sleep, reading is almost as restful. Don't wait until you have a free hour or two before taking time out. Fifteen minutes of complete relaxation taken two or three times a day is much more saving of your energy than two hours when you are restless and have frequent interruptions.

You need just as much patience and will power in gaining weight as the overweight person does in losing weight. Sometimes your problem is even greater because you have to dig out some of your unconscious and deep-seated pride or satisfaction in being underweight. You have to replace this with intelligent recognition of the need for normal weight and the advantages of increased vitality, better appearance, and greater stamina.

There is no special seven-day diet for you as there is for the overweight person. Why? Because when you look at the kind of diet that is usually given for an underweight person, you say, "Oh, I could never eat that much." And you're right; you can't hold large quantities of food, and you would be ill if you tried to stuff yourself willy-nilly.

You have two hurdles: first, to develop the habit of eating both the quantity and the kind of food you need for normal upkeep, and second, to add some extra calories for storage. Your problem requires specialized individual attention rather than a general diet. The directions below have been developed especially to help you clear these hurdles and land feet first on the side of normal weight.

For at least a week and maybe two, do just this:

Forget about calories and your weight.

Follow carefully the Daily Food Guide given in Chapter 9; omit nothing, but add anything you wish.

Find 15 minutes each day for extra rest.

If this applies to you, go slow on alcoholic beverages and other lone-wolf calories; also try not to smoke just before meals or at other times when smoking might dull your appetite.

THE COMMON SENSE WAY

When you start on a weight-gaining project, your aim is to add from 300 to 500 Calories a day to what you usually eat without feeling stuffed with food or being overwhelmed by what you need to eat to gain. Many of these extra calories must be accompanied by essential nutrients — protein, minerals, and vitamins. Adding just lone-wolf calories will not build the figure and feeling of well-being you are striving for. An underweight person needs to build additional muscle and supporting tissue and to improve the over-all functioning of the body as well as to deposit some fat.

You can include at least half of these extra calories in the foods you regularly eat if you use some food nuggets that are small in size but large in caloric and nutritive value. Here are a few you can practice adding inconspicuously:

Cheese or cheese-food

Count a 1-inch cube as about 100 Calories. Use it with mid-morning coffee instead of a cracker; put a sliver on poached or fried egg, a few slivers on a creamed vegetable, or with your usual sandwich fillings.

Count 1 tablespoon of cream cheese as 55 Calories.

Cream or fat

Count 1 tablespoon coffee cream as 30 Calories.

Count 1 tablespoon of heavy cream as 50 Calories. (For the calories in a teaspoon divide these figures by 3.)

Count 1 teaspoon of fat or oil or mayonnaise as 35 Calories.

Don't use so much that everything seems to be greasy. Mix it with the foods rather than just putting it on top or over the foods.

Mix with mashed potatoes, cereals, desserts.

Take a little more cream in coffee or tea.

Use oil dressing on your salad or a half teaspoon more butter or margarine on each slice of bread.

Milk

Undiluted evaporated milk:

Count 1 tablespoon as 22 Calories.

Add this to other milk dishes, 2 tablespoons in a custard, gravy, creamed vegetables, cereal cream or cooked cereal, mashed potato.

Dry milk:

Count 1 tablespoon of the instant nonfat milk solids as 12 to 18 Calories and 1 tablespoon of whole milk solids as about twice these amounts. These figures depend on the "dryness" of the milk solids. Caloric values usually are given on the label of the package.

Use this in powder form or reconstituted in the same way as you would use evaporated milk.

If you eat cooked cereal (farina, oatmeal, rice or others), instead of water cook it in milk—fresh, reconstituted evaporated or dry.

In the calorie column of the Table of Food Values (page 171) you will find other foods that will give you ideas for your new hobby of tucking in calories here and there.

It is likely that some of the extra 500 Calories will have to be more obvious. They may take the form of an additional half slice of bread or a serving of vegetables; a somewhat larger serving of dessert; a bedtime snack of fruit juice and a cracker with peanut butter; or salted nuts and small candies used after a meal or for a snack.

You may prefer to eat five or six small meals a day instead of the usual three. This is all right if they fit into your schedule of work and play. Three meals and some snacks, however, can do the job and is a more convenient plan for most people.

If 500 Calories seem too many for you to add to your usual food intake, start with 200 or 300 Calories, or even 100, and work up. Every extra calorie will help in gaining. Just be sure it is an *extra* calorie, for only then can it be stored to count toward your new weight.

Tobacco and alcohol can interfere with your eating enough of the foods you need for good health and normal weight. Drinking alcoholic beverages or smoking just before meals may satisfy your hunger and make you lose interest in food.

CALORIE ACCOUNTING

When you reach your desirable weight you will want to begin to drop out some of these extra 500 Calories. Omit about 100 Calories a day for a week and then wait a week before dropping another 100. If your weight goes down, put the calories back in your menus. If your weight stays up, you can try omitting a few more calories.

You would be wise to do a little honest bookkeeping of your calorie need and supply while you are tapering off the calories. First, write down how many calories a day you need for your desirable weight. Then write down the calorie value of everything you eat, as you eat it, and add it up as you go along. This gives you an up-to-the-minute record of how much you are supplying and reminds you how much you still have to supply before the end of the day. Calorie accounting like this will help you develop the habit of eating enough and will save you from the discouragement of losing weight again. You can stop counting calories as soon as your food habits can support this new weight.

Your weight will not need to be as much of a problem to you in the future as it has been in the past. Now you know how to keep it up. You will want to weigh often to check on how good your judgment is in matching your calorie supply to your calorie need — that is, in tailoring your appetite to insure both your fitness and your figure.

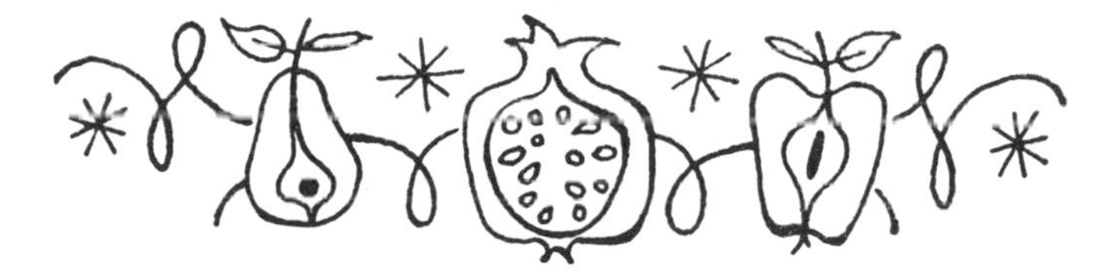

8.

The Nutrients

ENERGY IS AN ABSOLUTE NECESSITY, but to supply energy isn't the only reason we eat. We need materials for the body's growth, repair, and upkeep. During growth we must have large amounts of every kind of building material for muscle, bone, blood, vital organs, and other tissues. When growth is complete, smaller amounts of the same materials are needed for upkeep and repair. Also we need materials to regulate body processes, to keep everything about the body running in an efficient, orderly fashion.

All these different needs require different kinds of materials, called *nutrients*. There are at least fifty nutrients — many vitamins and minerals, amino acids from protein, fatty acids from fat, and starches and sugars.

Our plan of action to reach the goal of good eating and good health is first to choose foods containing calories which keep company with an abundance of these nutrients until all of our nutritional needs — except energy — have been supplied. After that we can choose calories from any source until our energy requirement is met.

To carry out this plan we need to know something more about foods than just their calorie values. If we choose our foods with thought for only their calorie values, we can wind up a day having had all the food our stomachs will hold, but obtaining very little nourishment for our health and vitality.

TOGETHERNESS!

Many of the nutrients occur together in our foods, and this fact greatly simplifies the job of selecting a nutritionally adequate diet.

Knowing about the nutrients, what foods supply them, and why we need them adds purpose and interest to our everyday eating habits.

You probably will recognize the names of the ten prominent nutrients as they are listed in the first column of the table on pages 88 and 89. Their special jobs in the building, upkeep, and operation of the body are listed in the second column. These are the jobs that cannot be done by other nutrients. Having an extra supply of one nutrient cannot make up for having a shortage of another. In addition to these individual jobs, there are also jobs, not described here, that require several nutrients to work together to perform some services for the body that no one nutrient can do alone.

The foods we can depend on to supply the nutrients, and their followers as well, are listed in the third column. As you study the chart you will notice:

Some foods can be grouped together because they supply important amounts of the same nutrients. For examples: breads and cereals; meat, fish, poultry, and eggs; milk, cheese, and ice cream.

Some foods supply important amounts of several of these ten leader nutrients. Some of these foods are: milk, cheese, meat, fish, poultry, and eggs.

Since no one group of foods supplies important amounts of all ten of the nutrients, it takes many kinds of food to supply all the dietary essentials for good health. This makes eating more interesting!

THESE, TOO

Here are just a few of the other nutrients which you hear mentioned frequently and which also do important jobs for a well-nourished, well-functioning body:

Phosphorus is needed in the soft tissues of the body and to combine with calcium to make bones and teeth. It is present in the foods that also supply protein and calcium.

Copper helps the body make iron into hemoglobin for the blood. It occurs in many foods.

Iodine is needed for the thyroid gland to make the hormone called thyroxin, which regulates the speed of some of the body processes. Iodine follows protein in sea food. Most of the iodine comes from the air, which picks it up from the sea, carries it overland, and drops it on the soil, on garden foods, and into water supplies. In areas such as the North Central States where there is no sea air, there is not enough iodine in the food, and iodized salt has been developed to supply this essential nutrient.

Fluorine helps the teeth resist decay. It is present in some water supplies and not others.

Niacin, a vitamin, is needed to maintain the health of the skin, tongue, and digestive system and to help the cells use oxygen. It is present in the foods that supply protein.

Folic acid, pyridoxine, pantothenic acid, and *vitamin B_{12}* are other essential vitamins that occur in many foods.

Water is an essential although people do not usually think of it as a food. We must have it to help carry nutrients to the cells, to carry waste products away, to build tissue, to regulate body temperature, to aid in digestion of food, to replace daily water loss, and to sustain the health of all body cells.

Scientists think it is most likely that foods contain other important nutrients which are as yet undiscovered. This is one of the many reasons why we need to get our nourishment from food instead of from vitamin and mineral pills or supplements which contain only the nutrients we know about.

Foods are the best sources of the nutrients we need. The grocery store, the meat market, the dairy, the bakery, the garden, the frozen food locker, and the food storage cellar are the supply houses of good nutrition.

HOW MUCH?

Good nutrition must concern itself with the *amounts* as well as with *kinds* of nutrients. Neither can substitute for the other. A large quantity of one nutrient cannot make up for the lack of another nutrient. The body must have a large enough supply of each nutrient to meet all of its different needs all of the time. A reserve supply of some nutrients in the body for use during emergencies is desirable also.

Recommendations for the amounts of different nutrients needed for good nutrition are made by a group of scientists who are members of the Food and Nutrition Board of the National Academy of Sciences-National Research Council. The Board has the responsibility for interpreting the results of research and setting up *Recommended Daily Dietary Allowances.* These are the amounts of calories and certain nutrients that are needed for the maintenance of good nutrition in healthy persons in the United States. Amounts are not specified for two of the nutrients (fats and carbohydrates) because supplying enough of these need not require special care in making food choices. The allowances are higher than the least amounts required for health; they provide a margin of safety for the nutrients but not for calories. They do not cover the additional requirements associated with disease or with recovery from malnutrition.

Recommended Daily Dietary Allowances

Designed for the Maintenance of Good Nutrition of Practically All Healthy Persons in the U.S.A.
(Allowances Are Intended for Persons Normally Active in a Temperate Climate)

Persons	Age in Years From	Age in Years Up to	Weight in Pounds	Height in Inches	Food Energy	Protein	Calcium	Iron	Vitamin A	Thiamine	Riboflavin	Ascorbic Acid	Vitamin D
					Calories	*Grams*	*Grams*	*Milligrams*	*International Units*	*Milligrams*	*Milligrams*	*Milligrams*	*International Units*
Men	18	35	154	69	2,900	70	.8	10	5,000	1.2	1.7	70	
	35	55	154	69	2,600	70	.8	10	5,000	1.0	1.6	70	
	55	75	154	69	2,200	70	.8	10	5,000	.9	1.3	70	
Women	18	35	128	64	2,100	58	.8	15	5,000	.8	1.3	70	
	35	55	128	64	1,900	58	.8	15	5,000	.8	1.2	70	
	55	75	128	64	1,600	58	.8	10	5,000	.8	1.2	70	
Pregnant (2nd and 3rd trimester)					+200	78	1.3	20	6,000	1.0	1.6	100	400
Lactating					+1,000	98	1.3	20	9,000	1.2	1.9	100	400
Children	1	3	29	34	1,300	32	.6	8	2,000	.5	.8	40	400
	3	6	40	42	1,600	40	.8	10	2,500	.6	1.0	50	400
	6	9	53	43	2,000	52	.8	12	3,500	.8	1.3	60	400
Boys	9	12	72	55	2,400	60	1.1	15	4,500	1.0	1.4	70	400
	12	15	98	61	3,000	75	1.4	15	5,000	1.2	1.8	80	400
	15	18	134	68	3,400	85	1.4	15	5,000	1.4	2.0	80	400
Girls	9	12	72	55	2,200	55	1.1	15	4,500	.9	1.3	80	400
	12	15	103	62	2,500	62	1.3	15	5,000	1.0	1.5	80	400
	15	18	117	64	2,300	58	1.3	15	5,000	.9	1.3	70	400

Adapted from Recommended Dietary Allowances, Sixth Revised Edition, 1964, Publication 1146. Prepared by Food and Nutrition Board, National Academy of Sciences—National Research Council, Washington, D.C. 20418.

Nutrient	*Some Reasons Why We Need It*	*Foods That Supply Important Amounts*
PROTEIN	To build and repair all tissues in the body To help form substances called antibodies which help fight infection To supply food energy	Meat, fish, poultry, eggs Milk, cheese Breads, cereals, other grain products Dry beans, dry peas Peanut butter, nuts
FAT	To supply a large amount of food energy in a small amount of food To supply substances called essential fatty acids	Butter, margarine, cream Salad oils, oil dressings Cooking fats, oils Peanut butter Bacon, other meat fats
CARBOHYDRATE (starches and sugars)	To supply food energy To help the body use other nutrients	Grain products, including breads, cereals, flours, cornmeal, rice, macaroni, spaghetti, noodles Potatoes, sweetpotatoes, corn Dried fruits, sweetened fruits, bananas Sugar, syrup, jelly, jam, honey
CALCIUM	To help build the bones and teeth To help blood to clot To help the muscles and nerves react normally	Milk, cheese (especially cheddar-type cheese), ice cream Collards, kale, broccoli, turnip and mustard greens
IRON	To combine with protein to make hemoglobin—the red substance that carries oxygen to the cells	Meat—liver, heart, and kidney are especially good sources Poultry, eggs, shellfish Dark green leafy vegetables, peas, beans Breads, cereals, and other grain products—whole grain, enriched or restored Dried fruits

Nutrient	*Some Reasons Why We Need It*	*Foods That Supply Important Amounts*
VITAMIN A	To help keep the skin and the mucous membrane (linings) of the nose, mouth, and inner organs healthy and resistant to infection To protect against night blindness	Dark green and deep yellow vegetables: broccoli, chard, collards, kale, spinach, turnip greens, other dark leaves; carrots, pumpkin, sweet potatoes, winter squash Apricots, cantaloup Liver, eggs, butter, margarine, cream
THIAMINE (vitamin B_1)	To keep the appetite and digestion normal To keep the nervous system healthy To help the body change certain substances in the food into energy for work and heat	Breads, cereals, other grain products whole-grain, enriched, or restored Meat, especially pork, liver, heart, and kidney Poultry and eggs Milk Peas, black-eyed peas, lima beans
RIBOFLAVIN (vitamin B_2)	To help the cells use oxygen To help keep vision clear To help keep the skin smooth and prevent scaly skin around the mouth and nose or cracking at the corners of the mouth	Milk, cheese, ice cream Meat, especially liver; poultry and eggs, fish Dark green vegetables Enriched bread, cereal products
VITAMIN C (Ascorbic acid)	To make a cementing substance that helps to hold body cells together and makes the walls of blood vessels firm To help resist infection To help in healing wounds and broken bones	Orange, grapefruit, other citrus fruits and juices, strawberries, cantaloup Tomatoes and tomato juice, green and red peppers Raw cabbage, broccoli, dark green leafy vegetables Potatoes and sweet potatoes, cooked in their jackets—especially new potatoes
VITAMIN D	To help the body absorb calcium from the digestive tract To help the body build strong bones and teeth	Milk with vitamin D added, eggs, butter Sardines, salmon, tuna Fish-liver oils

These recommended allowances are the goals toward which to work in planning adequate diets. They are also the goals used in planning our country's food supplies.

The Recommended Daily Dietary Allowances for men, women, and children of different ages are given in the table. An average height and weight is given for persons in each group.

The amounts of the different nutrients in this table are in the same terms — grams, milligrams, and International Units — as are the amounts present in the foods described in the Table of Food Values. A gram (abbreviated gm.) is smaller than an ounce; there are 28.4 grams in one ounce. There are one thousand milligrams (mg.) in one gram. An *International Unit* (abbreviated I.U.) is the measure of concentration or strength for vitamins A and D.

We can be well fed and have good food habits without knowing about this table of recommended allowances. It is given here to show the scientific basis for the Daily Food Guide which we do need to know about and which will be given in the next chapter. For this Guide the allowances have been translated into servings of the different foods which contain these nutrients. A *balanced diet* is the term often used for the combination of the right amounts of the right kinds of food to provide all of the nutrients in sufficient quantities for good health.

9.

A Daily Food Guide

One of the easiest, surest, and most pleasant ways to choose the food that best becomes us is to follow the Daily Food Guide that has been developed by food and nutrition specialists in the United States Department of Agriculture. It gives us as much choice as possible while still assuring us of a balanced diet. Also it gives us a good deal of free choice in selecting some of our calories.

All of the different kinds of foods have been sorted into four broad groups on the basis of their similarity in composition and nutritive value. Then the Guide specifies the number of servings we need from each food group to supply the recommended allowances for the many nutrients.

On the following pages is the Daily Food Guide — a guide for fitness.

To use this Daily Food Guide:

Select the main part of your diet from these four broad food groups.

Choose at least the number of servings recommended from each group.

Follow the suggestions given for the choices within each group.

Sizes of servings may differ — small for young children, extra large (or seconds) for very active adults or teen-agers. Expectant and nursing mothers also require additional servings, and these will be discussed in later chapters.

BREAD-CEREAL GROUP

Foods Included

All breads and cereals that are whole grain, enriched, or restored; check labels to be sure.

Specifically, this group includes: breads, cooked cereals, ready-to-eat cereals, cornmeal, crackers, flour, grits, macaroni and spaghetti, noodles, rice, rolled oats, quick breads and other baked goods if made with whole-grain or enriched flour.

Amounts Recommended

Choose 4 servings or more daily. Or, if no cereals are chosen, have an extra serving of breads or baked goods, which will make at least 5 servings from this group daily.

Count as 1 serving: 1 slice of bread; 1 ounce ready-to-eat cereal; ½ to ¾ cup cooked cereal, cornmeal, grits, macaroni, noodles, rice, or spaghetti.

MEAT GROUP

Foods Included

Beef, veal, lamb, pork, variety meats such as liver, heart, kidney

Poultry and eggs

Fish and shellfish

As alternates — dry beans, dry peas, lentils, nuts, peanuts, peanut butter

Amounts Recommended

Choose 2 or more servings every day.

Count as a serving: 2 to 3 ounces of lean, cooked meat; poultry or fish — all without bone; 2 eggs; 1 cup cooked dry beans, dry peas, or lentils; 4 tablespoons peanut butter.

MILK GROUP

Foods Included

Milk: fluid whole, evaporated, skim, dry, buttermilk

Cheese: cottage, cream, cheddar-type (natural or processed)

Amounts Recommended

Some milk every day for everyone.

Recommended amounts are given below in terms of whole fluid milk:

	8-ounce cups
Children under 9	3 to 4
Children 9 to 12	3 or more
Teen-agers	4 or more
Adults	2 or more
Pregnant women	4 or more
Nursing mothers	4 or more

Part or all of the milk may be fluid skim milk, buttermilk, evaporated milk, or dry milk.

Cheese and ice cream may replace part of the milk. The calcium content of the food is the basis for figuring the amount it will take to replace a given amount of milk. Common portions of various kinds of cheese and of ice cream and their milk equivalents in calcium are:

1-inch cube cheddar-type cheese	= ½ cup milk
½ cup cottage cheese	= ⅓ cup milk
2 tablespoons cream cheese	= 1 tablespoon milk
½ cup ice cream	= ¼ cup milk

VEGETABLE-FRUIT GROUP

Foods Included

All vegetables and fruits. This guide emphasizes those that are valuable as sources of vitamin C and vitamin A.

SOURCES OF VITAMIN C: *Good sources*: grapefruit or grapefruit juice, orange or orange juice, cantaloup, raw strawberries, broccoli, green pepper. Also guava, mango, papaya, sweet red pepper.

(Lemon juice has the same vitamin C content as orange and grapefruit juice, but usually is used in much smaller amounts.)

Fair sources: honeydew melon, lemon juice, tangerines or tangerine juice, watermelon, asparagus tips, raw cabbage, collards, garden cress, kale, kohlrabi, mustard greens, potatoes and sweet potatoes cooked in the jacket, spinach, tomatoes or tomato juice, turnip greens.

SOURCES OF VITAMIN A: Dark-green and deep-yellow vegetables and a few fruits, namely: apricots, broccoli, cantaloup, carrots, chard, collards, cress, kale, mango, persimmon, pumpkin, spinach, sweet potatoes, turnip greens and other dark-green leaves, winter squash.

Amounts Recommended

Choose 4 or more servings every day; these should include:

1 serving of a good source of vitamin C or 2 servings of a fair source

1 serving, at least every other day, of a good source of vitamin A

The remaining 1 to 3 or more servings may be of any vegetable or fruit, including potato.

Count as 1 serving: ½ cup of vegetable or fruit; or a portion as ordinarily served, such as 1 medium apple, banana, orange, or potato, or half of a medium grapefruit or cantaloup.

OTHER FOODS

Choose additional foods to add enough calories to complete, but *not to exceed,* your food energy needs for the day. These foods may come both from the different groups and from foods not listed.

Everyone will use some foods not specified (butter, margarine, other fats, oils, sugars, or unenriched refined grain products). These are often ingredients in baked goods and mixed dishes. Fats, oils, and sugars are also added to foods during preparation or at the table to enhance flavor and increase appetite appeal.

These "other foods" supply calories and can add to total nutrients in meals. They are a part of daily meals even though they are not stressed.

VARIETY IS IMPORTANT

Variety, especially in flavor, is a valuable ingredient in all of our meals. We don't want all of the foods to taste sweet or all of them to taste tart, or strong-flavored, or bland. It is the combination with interesting accents and blends that we enjoy.

Variety in the texture of the foods adds great interest to the meal. The crispness of a green salad or raw vegetables is good with the smoothness of mashed potatoes or other cooked vegetables. Lightly cooked vegetables have a semi-crisp texture which is different from the softness of long-cooked vegetables.

Variety in color pleases both the eye and the appetite. For this the colored vegetables and fruits are especially helpful. The temperatures of different foods in the same meal can add variety, as can the shape or form of a serving on a plate.

The best kind of variety is that which is built into good meals as they are planned, however simple the meals may be. It is not a window dressing of frills and fanciness which is added as an afterthought.

Most of the good modern cookbooks devote a good deal of space to meal planning and suggestions for the kinds of foods to serve together for different kinds of meals.

Despite its importance, variety is no substitute for quality. We want food that tastes good, smells good, and looks good!

FROM GUIDE TO MEALS

Arranging foods from the Daily Food Guide into three meals is easy; they almost arrange themselves. Starting with the groups for which the most servings are recommended, we would have:

Bread or some breadstuff or cereal at each meal, and some meals might have both bread and cereal.

Milk for children at each meal and milk for adults usually at two of the meals.

At least one serving from the vegetable-fruit group at each meal. Because our conventional breakfast menu includes fruit, this is one good time to serve the citrus fruit or some other chief source of vitamin C. It could, of course, be served at another meal or for a snack. The three or more other servings from the vegetable-fruit group could then be divided between the noon and evening meals.

One of the servings from the meat group at the evening meal and the other at the noon meal or breakfast, or divided between them. We do need a serving from either the milk group or the meat group at each of the three meals. Often we choose to have a serving of both.

This arrangement of the servings from the Daily Food Guide makes a basic menu pattern which is easy to follow when selecting our meals. It is equally useful when we are planning and preparing meals at home or when eating out and buying our meals ready-made.

BASIC MENU PATTERN FOR AN ADULT

This pattern is not a complete daily menu. It is an assortment of foods that will supply the major part of your needs for good nutrition. To this you can add other foods to round out your meals, or to use for snacks, and to satisfy your calorie need.

Food Group	*Number of Servings**	*Example of the Kind of Food*
BREAKFAST		
Vegetable-Fruit		
A good source of vitamin C	1	Grapefruit—½
Bread-Cereal	2	Toast Ready-to-eat cereal
Meat *or*	½	Egg—one
Milk	1	Milk—one cup
LUNCH OR SUPPER		
Meat	½ to 1	Luncheon meat
Bread-Cereal	1	Bread for sandwich
Vegetable-Fruit	1	Cabbage slaw or apple
Milk	1	Milk—one cup
DINNER		
Meat	1	Baked ham
Vegetable-Fruit		
A good source of vitamin A at least every other day	1	Mashed sweet potatoes
Other	1	Vegetable or fruit salad
Bread-Cereal	1	Hot biscuit
Milk (if not used at breakfast)	1	Milk—one cup

Also include some butter or margarine and other fat (see Chapter 10, Fats in Food).

The servings that are listed will supply between 1,300 and 1,600 Calories, depending upon the kinds of foods you choose from each food group.

*The size of servings is given in the Daily Food Guide, pages 93-97.

The Basic Menu does not list all of the food we need. It is the foundation of our total food intake for a day — a foundation of the right foods to become us. To this we can add more servings from the four food groups and other foods to round out our meals to suit our needs and preferences.

FOOD IN THE MORNING

Everyone needs to eat good food at the beginning of each day. "Eat a good breakfast to start a good day" is more than a slogan; it is a research fact. Studies have shown that people who eat a good breakfast are more alert and get more done than those who skip the morning meal. Even after lunch the breakfast skippers perk up for only the early part of the afternoon and then slow down again.

The body needs regular refueling and renourishing to be in top-notch working condition all of the time and to give us health and vigor. It is not like a machine that stops running as soon as the fuel tank is empty. When supplies are lacking, the body will cut down on whatever activities it can, but many living processes must be maintained continuously. For this it has to borrow from its cells, skimp along, and "make do" until food energy and nutrient supplies arrive.

Working all morning without eating breakfast is a little like spending money before we earn it — each meal or pay check must be used to pay off the accumulated debts instead of giving us some working capital for the time ahead. The coffee-break system in offices and factories has had an unfortunate effect on many people's breakfast habits and on their health, too. It has led them to substitute mid-morning coffee and a snack for breakfast. Yet the snack they choose often supplies chiefly lone-wolf calories.

Another reason for eating breakfast is to make a start on the important job of eating all of the foods we need each day. If we wait until noon to start, it is difficult to complete the job satisfactorily by the end of the day.

A good breakfast will include servings from at least three of the four food groups in the Daily Food Guide. A breakfast need not be heavy with calories to meet this specification although you do need some food energy to start the day. A half a grapefruit, a slice of toast with a teaspoon of butter or margarine, and a glass of skim milk or a boiled or poached egg would supply 225 to 300 Calories (305 to 380 Calories if you prefer to use whole milk). This is too short on food energy for starting the day unless your total energy need is very small indeed, or unless you are going to have a morning snack.

People differ in how much food they like or get accustomed to eating at the beginning of the day. If you have not been in the habit of eating breakfast, you may need to start with small servings and gradually work up to eating ordinary amounts of the important foods. You will be pleasantly surprised at how much better you will feel at the end of the day as well as at the beginning.

The food we eat in the morning does not need to conform to a conventional breakfast menu. Perhaps we are too unimaginative in choosing the food that "becomes us" at the start of the day. If you are tired of ordinary foods, why not have a new taste adventure? Try cheese and crackers, or baked custard made with only a little sugar, soups made with milk, cottage cheese served with fruit, a fried egg or egg salad sandwich, or a broiled cheese or hamburger sandwich.

For many who need lots of food at this meal, potatoes are still a favorite accompaniment of ham and eggs.

Whether you call it breakfast or "just eating something," whether you sit at a well-laid table or stand at the counter in your kitchen or at the drug store, be sure that some nutritious food becomes you as you start your day.

THE LATER YEARS

Having a long life is getting to be a habit with us. But many men and women with lots of birthdays behind them are not as healthy and happy as they would like to be and as they could be if they were wise eaters. Food becomes older people just as it does younger ones, but some oldsters seem to retire from their responsibility for being well fed.

Many of the common ills of older people — fatigue, depression, sleeplessness, worry, slow recovery from illness, and even overweight — often can be traced to poor food habits and a poor nutritional state. These handicaps can be removed when people have an adequate diet which provides the nutritional essentials needed for normal functioning of the adult body at every age.

Our bodies and the calendar do not always agree on when we begin to get old. Some people are still young when they are 70 years old, while others are old at 40. Age is judged more by activity, muscular coordination and agility, endurance, and by our attitudes and outlook on life, than by the number of years we have lived.

In the usual process of aging, our bodies function less efficiently and we have less strength and endurance as we approach and pass the three-score-and-ten milestone. The wise person adjusts his activities to a slower pace and learns to live within his physical budget while still enjoying life and having fun.

As activity decreases, less food energy is needed, but needs for protein, calcium, and the vitamins remain much the same. The Daily Food Guide is still our best standard, but we usually need to cut down on some of the extras, especially the lone-wolf calories. There is less room for sweets, fats, and rich gravies and desserts in our calorie budget than when we were younger.

Many people are not fortunate enough to have good teeth in later years when they particularly need to chew food thoroughly to aid in its digestion. The paring knife, the food chopper or blender, a little extra cooking to soften the sturdy fibers, and sometimes even the food strainer or sieve can substitute for the teeth of younger days. Often raw vegetables cause discomfort because of their rough-and-tumble capers in the intestinal tract. But the same vegetables after being cooked and mashed become dignified and important contributors toward supplying daily food needs. Raw fruits often are tolerated better than raw vegetables; and grinding or chopping meat is particularly helpful in making it ready for digestion.

Many older people need to eat more often than when they were younger. For them smaller meals and between-meal snacks are more suitable than the conventional three-squares-a-day.

An older person has to exert more effort to be well fed when living alone than when living with a family where generous meals are prepared routinely. People alone often slip into the habit of living on a very limited and inadequate diet — too many meals of just tea and toast or soup and crackers. Such poor food habits start a self-perpetuating merry-go-round of fatigue, physical and mental sluggishness, poor appetite, and lack of interest in food.

Starting early to form good food habits and then keeping them will add greatly to our good health in the pleasant, rewarding "later years."

10.

Fats in Food

MANY PEOPLE have been confused and worried about the possible relation of fat in the diet to atherosclerosis and certain kinds of coronary heart disease. There have been many hastily formed, inaccurate theories, and these have led to some unsound dietary recommendations. This chapter is written especially to explain what we do and do not know about the part played by diet and by other factors in our daily living in relationship to this disease. It also suggests what we can do to take advantage of the facts and leads that science has given us thus far.

First, a look at the normal aspects of fat in our diet: Fats are an important kind of food for all of us. In addition to adding variety and flavor to many foods, fats are concentrated sources of energy, suppliers of essential fatty acids, and carriers of vitamins A and D, E and K. Reasonable amounts of fat deposits are *needed* in the body to support and protect the vital organs and areas. A layer of fat under the skin is good insulation and protects the body from excessive loss of heat.

LINOLEIC ACID

One substance of particular importance which occurs in some fats is *linoleic acid.* (Chemically it is referred to as an essential unsaturated fatty acid.) Linoleic acid is needed for growth and reproduction, for a healthy skin, and for the body's proper use and storage of fat. A deficiency of linoleic acid interferes with the body's normal use of fat. The human body cannot make linoleic acid, so it must be supplied by the food we eat. Common foods which contain appreciable amounts of linoleic acid are the natural oils from corn, cottonseed, and soybean. Smaller amounts are found in peanut oil and poultry fat, and still smaller amounts in olive oil and pork fat. The fats of beef, lamb, milk, and coconut oil contain very little linoleic acid.

Margarines and the usual man-made shortenings differ widely in linoleic acid content, depending on the raw materials used and the extent to which hydrogen has been added to change some of the oils into solids or semi-solids. Adding hydrogen, a process called hydrogenation, changes linoleic acid into a substance that cannot do for the body what linoleic acid does.

Our daily requirement for linoleic acid is not known exactly but it is relatively small. There is, however, a little less linoleic acid in the average American diet today than there was 30 years ago.

Now a look at some of the problems: As most people grow older a fatty substance may be deposited inside the walls of the blood vessels. If this deposit clogs the vessels and interferes with the flow of blood, the condition is called atherosclerosis (one kind of arteriosclerosis). Often, but not always, with atherosclerosis there is also an increase in blood pressure. If the interference with blood circulation is severe enough, especially in the vessels close to the heart or in the brain, the result is a heart attack or a stroke. Probably heredity plays some part in the susceptibility of a person to atherosclerosis.

CHOLESTEROL

In the fatty deposits along the walls of the blood vessels there is a substance called *cholesterol.* Cholesterol is a normal constituent of blood, which the body uses in making other important substances it needs for normal functioning. Too much cholesterol in the circulating blood has been blamed for causing atherosclerosis and leading to heart attacks, but conclusive scientific evidence for this is lacking.

The amount of cholesterol in the blood of normal persons varies within wide limits. Not everyone who has more than an average amount of cholesterol in his blood has atherosclerosis. Also not everyone who has atherosclerosis has more than an average amount of cholesterol in his blood.

The body makes cholesterol whether or not it is present in the food we eat, so the amount of cholesterol in the food we eat probably is not of major importance in determining the amount of cholesterol in our blood. Low cholesterol diets have received considerable attention but we have not yet been able to measure how useful they are. A diet low in cholesterol limits the selection of highly nutritious foods such as meat, eggs, cheese, and milk and can lead to an imbalance or a deficiency of nutrients.

There is some evidence that fats with a high content of linoleic acid may help to reduce high levels of cholesterol in the blood. However, we lack positive evidence that reducing the amount of cholesterol in the blood reduces the occurrence of atherosclerosis.

Studies with laboratory animals suggest that the way the body uses fat may be related to the kind of carbohydrate in the diet. When different kinds of carbohydrates were fed to rats, the more complex chemical units of starch seemed to permit the body's normal use of fat better than the simpler chemical units of sucrose (ordinary sugar), or of glucose (sometimes called dextrose and found in syrups and many other foods). These are only preliminary results and their application to human nutrition is yet to be proven. Studies of the average American diet over the last 50 years show a steady increase in the amount of sugar, and a decrease in the amount of starch.

PERSONAL CONTROL

Research eventually will give us definite answers and detailed recommendations to help in the prevention and treatment of some of these difficulties. In the meantime we have many leads to things we can do to avoid or lessen trouble and to improve our resistance to abnormal conditions of any kind. Almost every phase of our living — food, weight, exercise, rest, and emotions — seems to be involved in some way directly or indirectly with atherosclerosis and coronary heart disease. They are all items over which we can have a good deal of control if we choose.

We *can eat* the kinds and amounts of food that science has proven we need in order to be well nourished — in other words a well-balanced diet. We *should not omit* any one kind of food, or *use any to excess.* For instance, using no corn or cottonseed or soybean oils would be omitting our chief source of linoleic acid. On the other hand, using too much of these concentrated sources of food energy would be adding calories unnecessarily.

We *can include* some kinds of fat in our diet each day to supply linoleic acid. The amount of linoleic acid in a tablespoon of a corn, cottonseed, or soybean oil, or in twice that amount of peanut oil or chicken fat, plus what is present in the other foods we eat, probably is a generous daily supply.

Salad and cooking oils made from corn, cottonseed, and soybean oils are available in most markets and are labelled as to the kind they contain. Ordinary cooking temperatures do not harm linoleic acid, but high temperatures that cause any fat or oil to smoke are undesirable. Commercial dressings, such as mayonnaise and French dressing are made most often with one of these three oils or with blends of them.

We *can avoid* overeating for our level of physical activity and thus avoid excess calories and overweight. This means choosing our calories by the nutrient company they keep, and limiting our intake of foods which provide little except calories. Fortunately the foods which often are needed to improve the nutritional quality of our diets — milk and fruits and vegetables — are low in calories in relation to the other chief nutrients they supply.

We *can organize* our lives to include some regular physical activity that will use the larger muscles and keep them firm and agile. This needs to be more than the usual sitting, standing, walking a few steps, and then sitting again, that so many of us have as our daily routine. The activity may be as mild as walking or as strenuous as swimming but it should be suitable for our strength and vigor. The importance of exercise to good health and weight control has been discussed in Chapter 4 on Activity and Calories. We find evidence in the medical literature that persons whose muscles are in reasonably good condition are less likely to suffer from heart disease than those whose daily routine includes only very limited physical effort.

We *can strive* for emotional stability or balance. Emotions can influence every part of the body and the way it operates. Constant worry, tension, fatigue, apprehension, even too great or unrealistic ambitions, handicap both the mind and the body in functioning normally with the greatest sense of well-being. Good nutrition at every age contributes to emotional stability.

Every one regardless of his age can profit from observing such common-sense rules as these for good health and good living.

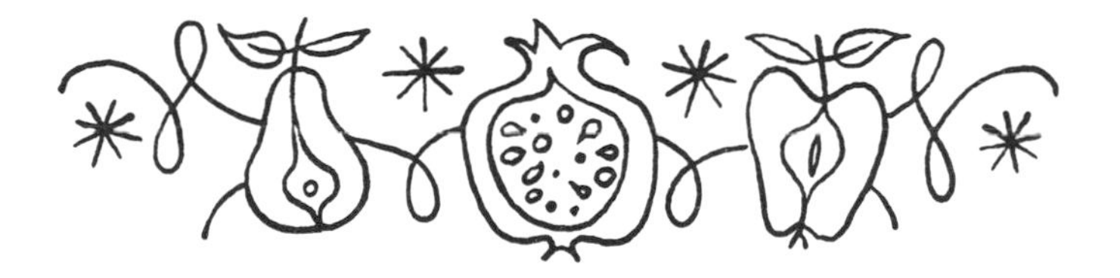

11.

Parents-in-Waiting

THIS CHAPTER is written for a special group of readers — the men and women who are going to be fathers and mothers. It is the woman who supplies the materials for the baby's growth, but the father, too, wants to know what makes a healthy mother and child. His understanding of their food needs is an important step toward taking a share of the responsibilities of parenthood and becoming a good father. Nothing can help the expectant mother more!

Normal as is the process of having a baby, it does make extra nutritional demands on the mother's body. Research studies have shown repeatedly the relation between the quality of a mother's diet and her health during pregnancy, the condition of her baby at birth and for weeks and months after birth, and her ability to breast-feed him. A good diet protects her health and helps to make a healthy happy baby. It also helps to prepare the mother's body for the important work of producing milk for the baby.

So much for generalities — now let's talk about *you.* "You" means the mother, because it is her food needs that interest us, and "us" includes the fathers.

Now your food will become the baby, too. The blood stream is the only connection between you and your baby, and through this must pass all the materials that become the baby. From the food you eat you can supply enough for his growth and development without having to use any of your own body materials or stores of nutrients and energy. There is no nerve connection between you and your baby, so your ideas, impressions, and emotions are not transferred to the baby. He is, however, affected by your fatigue or worry when they interfere with your food supply or its availability to him.

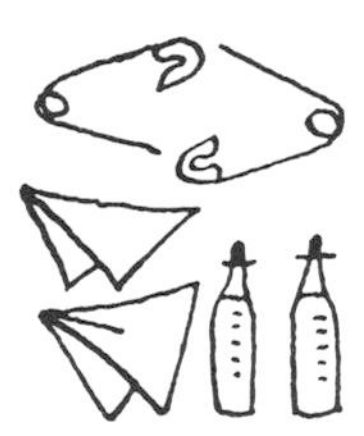

Your food needs are not the same during all nine months of pregnancy. As the baby grows and becomes more active and as your body prepares for the work of producing milk for him, your food needs increase gradually. The nine months are usually divided into 3 three-month periods called trimesters.

THE FIRST MONTHS

You can chart your food course through a healthy expectancy by the Daily Food Guide which has been given with a basic menu pattern in the previous chapter. If you were following the Guide carefully before you became pregnant, then you will not need to make any changes during the first three or four months.

If, however, your usual food choices did not include the recommended amounts from the different food groups, such as milk, or fruits rich in vitamin C, or vegetables rich in vitamin A, then it is urgent that you begin immediately to eat these regularly. Also, it would be wise to use some extra servings of any of the important foods which you have been slighting.

Are you still a teen-ager? One-fourth of the mothers having their first babies are in this age group. Then use the Basic Menu Pattern given on page 152 for teen-agers in order to help provide the nutrients you need to complete your own growth and development.

As important as anything during the first few months is for the parents-in-waiting to check up on their food habits. Ask yourselves if you are eating the kinds and amounts of foods that science has proven are essential for good health and fitness at every age. Are your ideas about food and the importance of good nutrition correct and up-to-date, or do you let food fads and prejudices keep you from eating wisely? Will your food habits set a good example for your child so he can be guided toward a lifetime of wise eating for good health? How do you rate on "willingness to eat" as described in Chapter 2? You may find that you need to work on improving some of your food habits. Parents can be counted on to be heroes in an emergency, but many parents are cowards when faced with eating foods they don't like, or think they don't like, or aren't used to. Their poor example often is responsible for a child's becoming a feeding problem.

During pregnancy some women develop cravings for certain foods, but these are not an indication of nutritional need. These cravings can be humored unless they become unreasonable or interfere with good food habits. Then they would be a health hazard.

Some women have trouble with nausea or morning sickness early in pregnancy. Usually, eating several snacks during the day is helpful in preventing and overcoming this. The best snacks are small ones which include some solid food such as crackers or bread or fruit and a small amount of milk or fruit juice. The snacks must count nutritionally because, if you need two or three snacks a day for a few weeks, you will need to eat less at mealtime or you will gain unwanted weight.

GAINING WEIGHT

Your doctor will tell you how much or how little you may gain during the nine months. Most doctors allow a total gain of 18 to 25 pounds, depending on your body build. Only if you are underweight will you want to gain weight during the first three months of your pregnancy. (If you are overweight, it is safe for you to lose a few pounds, if you do it by leaving out of your diet only the lone-wolf calories.) An average gain of one-half pound a week is usually permitted during the fourth, fifth, and sixth months. Then during the last three months it may be all right for you to have an average gain of a pound or a pound and a quarter a week.

If you are a small, inactive person you may have a hard time keeping your weight gain down to what your doctor considers desirable. As you follow the Daily Food Guide you will have to skip second servings of the foods listed in the Basic Menu Pattern. You will need to: use skim milk rather than whole milk (1 glass skim milk supplies 90 Calories; 1 glass whole milk supplies 160 Calories), use very small amounts of fats, and omit sweets and other lone-wolf calories. Of course, you will already have many of these habits if you are a small, inactive person who has learned to avoid being overweight!

THE LAST HALF

About the fourth month of pregnancy your food needs begin to increase. From the fourth to the ninth months you require more of most of the chief nutrients and more food energy. During the seventh, eighth, and ninth months your baby triples his weight and in every way gets more and more ready to be born and to live an independent life. This is the time also when you want to get ready nutritionally to nurse your baby because this can give him the best possible start in life.

You do not need to "eat for two" as the old saying would have you believe, but your nutritional needs will increase. You need half again as much calcium and vitamin C, a third more protein, riboflavin, iron, and some additional vitamin A and thiamine, than you did before pregnancy. You will also need more vitamin D.

Your calorie need increases less than any of these nutrients — only 10 or at the very most 20 per cent! You surely have to choose your calories by the company they keep — adding foods that supply lots of different nutrients without adding many calories. The Basic Menu Pattern, like your clothes, needs to be expanded for the months ahead to supply larger amounts of the important foods for growth and fitness.

Milk is the surest way to add the extra calcium and riboflavin you need, and it will also provide the extra protein. The Guide specifies 3 cups of milk for you now. However, if you are an expectant teen-ager 3 cups are not enough. You need 3 cups a day just to finish your own body building and maturation. Adding another cup of milk will supply the needs of your baby-to-be. Of course, some of the milk may be included as cheese and ice cream.

For your increased vitamin C need, add another serving of a good source of this vitamin or two extra servings of a fair source.

For added vitamin A, thiamine, and iron, choose dark-green leafy vegetables. The Daily Food Guide recommends a serving of these or deep-yellow vegetables at least every other day. Now you will need to choose a serving almost every day, and favor the green leafy ones which also supply iron.

If you like liver, or can learn to like it, use it once a week. It is packed with many nutrients but especially iron, vitamin A, and riboflavin as well as protein.

BASIC MENU FOR THE LAST 6 MONTHS OF PREGNANCY

This pattern is not a complete daily menu. It is an assortment of foods that will supply the major part of your needs for good nutrition. To this you can add other foods to round out your meals or snacks and to satisfy your calorie need.

Food Group	*Number of Servings**	*Example of the Kind of Food*
BREAKFAST		
Vegetable-Fruit		
A good source of vitamin C	1	Grapefruit
Bread-Cereal	2	Oatmeal Toast
Milk	1	Milk—one cup
SNACK—MORNING OR AFTERNOON		
Bread-Cereal	1	Crackers
Milk	1	Milk—one cup
LUNCH OR SUPPER		
Meat	1	Tuna fish
Vegetable-Fruit	1	Raw vegetable salad
Bread-Cereal	1	Bread
Milk	1	Milk—one cup
DINNER		
Meat	1	Roast pork
Vegetable-Fruit		
A good source of vitamin A almost every day	1	Broccoli
Other	1	Browned potato
Bread-Cereal	1	Hot roll
BEDTIME SNACK		
Vegetable-Fruit		
A good source of vitamin C	1	Orange juice
Bread-Cereal	1	Plain cookie or crackers

Also include some butter or margarine and other fat (see Chapter 10, Fats in Food).

The servings that are listed will supply between 1,750 and 2,050 Calories, depending upon the kind of foods you choose from each food group. Using skim milk in place of whole milk will reduce the calories by about 210 Calories.

* The size of servings is given in the Daily Food Guide section, pages 93–97.

You may not get enough vitamin D from food alone unless you regularly use whole milk which has been fortified with this vitamin (400 I.U. per quart). The vitamin D you get from sunshine varies with the season and with how much your skin is exposed to direct sunlight. Your doctor may give you a prescription for a vitamin D concentrate.

Good food for the mother during pergnancy has far-reaching benefits. It safeguards her health for the present and for the future. This in turn increases the joys of motherhood and the possibility of her nursing her baby. The right food for the mother gives the baby the best possible start toward a healthy happy life. Also, if it has not been present before, the habit of eating well becomes established in the family and everyone benefits.

Your next interest is in supplying the baby with the food that becomes him best after he is born — mother's milk. The chapter ahead tells you how you can build on the foundation of good nutrition during pregnancy and be successful in nursing your baby.

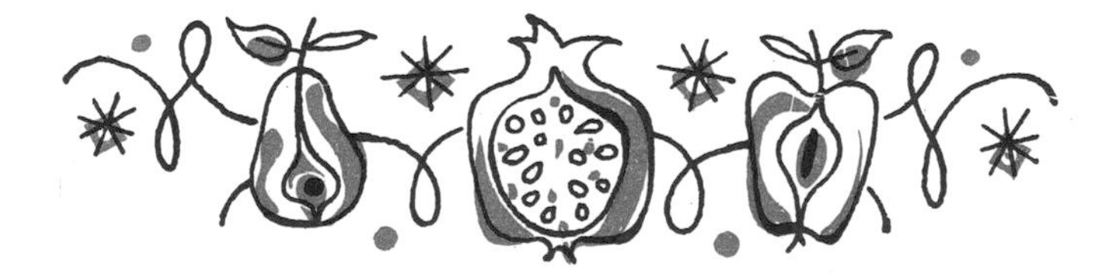

12.

Food for the Baby

BREAST FEEDING YOUR BABY is an important stage in the sequence of events of motherhood. The responsibilities of the mother's body do not end with the birth of her baby. They go on even more intensively during the nursing period. Now you actually can see, as well as know, how vital you are to your baby. Many medical authorities consider that breast feeding has highly important physiological and psychological values to both mother and baby.

Whether or not you can nurse your baby successfully depends chiefly on your health, your diet before and after the baby is born, and your interest and satisfaction in being able to nurse him.

AT THE HOSPITAL

Sometimes the rigid schedule of the hospital prevents the early relationship of mother and infant which is needed to start satisfactory milk production and nursing. For a closer personal relationship between mother and baby, some hospitals are keeping a baby in the same room with his mother instead of in a nursery. This is called a "rooming-in" plan. A mother is more likely to have plenty of milk if she has the satisfaction and pleasure of holding and loving the baby often, taking care of him, and feeding him whenever he is hungry than if she sees and feeds him only by a hospital schedule.

If you do not have enough milk for the baby while you are in the hospital, try not to be discouraged. This alone can reduce your milk supply. You can look forward to having more milk after you go home with your baby and are able to care for him and yourself.

VERY SPECIAL

Nothing can quite equal the advantages of breast feeding when mother and baby are healthy. Milk from a healthy mother is more easily digested and thus less likely to cause digestive upsets than the usual formulas of bottle-fed babies. Mother's milk is always the right temperature, it is free of harmful bacteria, and it is more economical of the mother's time and energy.

For the first three or four days after the baby is born,

the secretion of the breasts is not milk but a substance called *colostrum*. Colostrum is of very special value to the newborn infant as he starts to nourish his own body because it contains more protein and salts than milk, as well as certain substances which give the baby resistance to infection; also, it acts as a laxative. For about two weeks the milk keeps some of the qualities of this colostrum.

No mother should feel that all is lost if she cannot or does not nurse her baby. She can do several things to compensate for feeding her baby by bottle and formula (which the doctor has prescribed). When giving him his bottle she should cuddle him close as though she were breast feeding him. This will give him the necessary sense of nearness and belonging. She should allow plenty of time so that she can feel unhurried and relaxed and enjoy this time with her baby. The spirit in which she feeds him counts as well as the kind of milk she gives him.

FOOD FOR TWO

A baby requires more of all the nutrients and food energy after he is born. He needs energy for his own breathing, his heart action, muscle tone, and all of his activity. His body is made up of very active tissue, and he is growing faster than he ever will again. He needs 45 to 50 Calories for each pound each day during his first year. Contrast this with your own requirement of about 16 to 20 Calories for each pound! Now you need more food to nurse your baby successfully than you needed for his growth before he was born.

Compared with the dietary allowances for you before

you were pregnant, your food should supply about two-thirds more of most of the nutrients – protein, calcium, vitamins A and C, riboflavin, and thiamine – and about one-third more of iron and calories.

Your daily food selections must now include additional servings of the food groups which are the chief sources of these nutrients.

To supply the extra calcium, protein, and riboflavin you now need to *add* 2 cups of milk, which means a total of 4 cups of milk each day. You can eat cheese and ice cream to supply some of this amount.

To supply more vitamin C you now need to *add* 1 serving of a fruit that is a good source of this vitamin. This means a total of 2 servings each day. You can eat fair sources of vitamin C to supply some of this vitamin, but it takes 2 of these servings to replace 1 serving of a good source.

To supply more vitamin A you need a serving of dark-green or deep-yellow vegetable every day.

To meet your increased demands for the other nutrients and for calories choose more servings from the Bread-Cereal Group and the Meat Group. You need to include plenty of water and other liquids too.

Now the Basic Menu Pattern for you must include all of these servings of the foods which are so important to you and your baby. As with the other patterns, it is the foundation of your daily diet. You will need to add other foods and more of the same foods until your need for energy is supplied.

If you are still a teen-ager, add the extra servings specified from the four food groups to the Basic Menu Pattern given for you in Chapter 14. Then your food

BASIC MENU PATTERN FOR A NURSING MOTHER

This pattern is not a complete daily menu. It is an assortment of foods that will supply the major part of your needs for good nutrition. To this you can add other foods to round out your meals or snacks and to satisfy your calorie need.

Food Group	*Number of Servings**	*Example of the Kind of Food*
BREAKFAST		
Vegetable-Fruit		
A good source of vitamin C	1	Grapefruit juice
Bread-Cereal	2	Cereal
		Toast
Meat	½	Egg
Milk	1	Milk—one cup
MORNING SNACK		
Milk	½	Cheese—one-inch cube
Bread-Cereal	½	Graham crackers
LUNCH OR SUPPER		
Meat	1	Ground beef pattie
Bread-Cereal	1	Bread
Vegetable-Fruit	1	Cabbage
Milk	1	Milk—one cup
AFTERNOON SNACK		
Vegetable-Fruit		
A good source of vitamin C	1	Orange
Bread-Cereal	½	Crackers
DINNER		
Meat	1	Roast lamb
Vegetable-Fruit		
A good source of vitamin A every day	1	Spinach
Other	2	Scalloped potatoes
		Raw vegetable or fruit salad
Bread-Cereal	1	Hot roll
Milk	½	Milk—one-half cup
		¼ serving in scalloped potatoes
		¼ serving as ice cream
BEDTIME SNACK		
Milk	1	Chocolate milk—one cup

Also include some butter or margarine and other fat (see Chapter 10, Fats in Foods).

The servings that are listed will supply between 2,000 to 2,300 Calories, depending upon the kinds of foods you choose from each food group. Using skim milk in place of whole milk will reduce the calories by about 230 Calories.

* The size of servings is given in the Daily Food Guide section, beginning on page 93.

will supply enough body-building materials for both you and your baby.

Snacks between meals and at bedtime are advisable for refueling and renourishing your body. They also help you include all of the foods you need every day without having to crowd too much food into each meal.

The quality of your milk depends on the food you eat and on the stores of nutrients you have in your body. The supplies of protein and calcium that you stored during pregnancy will be used now. You need them in addition to the large amounts supplied daily by the food you eat. Your doctor may prescribe vitamin D for both you and the baby. Also, he probably will have you give the baby a little orange juice for extra vitamin C beginning some time during the first month.

CALORIES FOR TWO

Your total calorie need changes as the baby grows. Your food should supply enough calories to keep your weight normal plus enough for the milk the baby needs to thrive on.

From the information on page 87 find how many calories you need daily for your size and activity level. To this need, add 800 to 1,000 Calories for the production of milk. Experience, and weighing of yourself as well as the baby frequently, will guide you in knowing how much extra to eat. You will need to eat as much as you possibly can without gaining weight.

When part of the milk the baby needs is provided by a formula and you are producing only the remaining part, you will need fewer calories than if you were supplying all of the milk.

FACTS FOR YOU

Your doctor can tell you many things about your milk and its production that will help you to be successful in nursing your baby. For instance, nursing stimulates milk secretion; also, emptying the breast completely at each nursing stimulates secretion. The accumulation of milk in the breast, however, discourages secretion. Heavy work, fatigue, or lack of sleep also reduce the secretion. Your milk is richer in the morning after a night's rest than at night after a day's activity. For this reason you may need to shorten the time between nursings or let the baby nurse a little longer at feedings toward the end of the day.

The flavor of spices and condiments in your food is transferred to your milk and may upset the baby. You will want to avoid these. Occasionally, strong-flavored vegetables such as onions and cauliflower are troublesome in the same way.

Emotional factors have a great influence on your ability to produce milk for your baby. Being worried or excited or getting too tired interferes with both the quantity and quality of your milk. But being calm, happy, and affectionate stimulates milk production.

BABY KNOWS

Babies differ in how much and how often they need to be fed. For this reason their schedules need to be personalized. A personalized schedule does not mean feeding a baby every time he cries, but it does mean considering him as an individual who wants to be comfortable and happy but cannot be when he is hungry or thirsty. It means respecting a certain amount of variation in his hunger and appetite and not insisting on too rigid a feeding pattern either in the amount he eats or in the time between feedings.

A healthy baby is a better judge of when he needs food than a clock is. He will develop a fairly regular daily schedule when he is getting enough to eat, whether breast fed or bottle fed. The schedule may start at a different time each day, but the time between feedings will be similar from day to day. If he is hungry during the night, he needs to be fed and will let you know. He will break himself of a night feeding when he no longer needs such frequent refueling. But when he is not fed during the night, he is hungrier when he wakes up, so he needs to be fed promptly. The first two feedings in the morning may need to be quite close together.

A hungry baby spends a good share of his life expressing his outrage at the clock and the people who watch it instead of him. Persistent crying does not always mean that he has colic; it may be his expression of anger at not being fed when he needs food.

The doctor will tell you when to add other foods to the baby's diet. The amounts must be kept small, especially for the first six months. When a baby is fed too much of the solid foods, he may lose his interest in milk and not take enough of it. Also he may eat too much and be fat. New foods must never take the place of any of the milk he needs.

You probably will wean the baby some time after he is six months old. Even if you have nursed him for only a month or two, both of you have benefited. After the baby is weaned, you will have to eat less — only enough food for your own body now — or you will gain weight!

AN ANSWER BOOK

For the months ahead you will want a reliable book on infant care and feeding. There are several excellent ones and some of them are available in inexpensive paper-bound editions. Ask your doctor to recommend one. Such a book will answer many of the questions you need or want to ask, particularly with your first baby; then you can call your doctor for answers to the special questions.

13.

The First Dozen Years

CHILDREN LIKE TO EAT, and they develop good food habits from having satisfying experiences with the foods they need for growth and with the people who are providing these foods.

The importance of good food habits, the body's need for many different nutrients, and how these nutrients can be supplied by our daily food have been discussed in previous chapters. This information applies to the first dozen years as well as to the later ones.

The total daily amount of food energy, protein, minerals, and vitamins that a child needs increases steadily, but not rapidly, as he grows through his first dozen years. During his first two or three years he grows faster and needs more food for his size than at any later time in his life. Sometimes after his second birthday he begins to grow more slowly and needs fewer calories in proportion to his size. This slower rate continues until he is about 9 or 10 years old; then it begins to speed up and stays at a more rapid rate until he is somewhere in his mid or late teens.

The erroneous idea that because a child is growing he needs more food than an adult, has led many parents to overfeed their children. This is likely to cause "feeding problems" and sometimes overweight. Not until a boy is 12 or 14 years old is he likely to need as many total calories each day as his father; after that age, and until he is grown, he needs more. Not until a girl is 13 or 14 does she need as much as her mother, and then her need has reached its peak and goes no higher. No child should be permitted to form the habit of eating more than he needs. His weight gain in relation to his height is a good indication of whether his food is supplying the right amount of total calories.

Until a child is 10 to 12 years old his total daily requirements for protein, most vitamins, and iron are *smaller* than those for an adult. (But, like his calorie requirement, these are larger in proportion to his size than for an adult.) His requirements for minerals, calcium, phosphorus, and for vitamin D, however, are *larger* than for the adults. There is no nutritional substitute for milk in supplying these important minerals for building strong straight bones. Unless the child is getting a great deal of sunshine every month of the year, the doctor will recommend a supplement of vitamin D for the preschool years at least.

The Daily Food Guide for the first dozen years includes more milk and smaller servings of the other food groups than for the adults. Also, in the early years of this age group the flavor of the food will be milder and its consistency smoother, and feeding times may be more frequent than in the later years. The servings need to be very small for the toddler and should increase in size very gradually. As he grows and requires more food, larger or additional servings from *all* of the food groups are needed to supply enough of the essential nutrients. Giving him larger servings only of meat and not of other important foods — milk, vegetables and fruits, breads and cereals — will not provide him with an adequate diet nor help him to form the best food habits.

NEW FLAVORS

Usually children are keenly aware of the flavor and texture and temperature of food. The young child prefers plain food, simply cooked and easy to eat. He prefers mild flavors and smooth, tender textures. He does not like either cooked or raw vegetables that are coarse or stringy. He is sensitive to the temperature of his food and does not want it very hot or cold. He wants his soup cool and his ice cream melted, and urging him to eat something while it is still hot, or before it melts, may interfere with his enjoyment of it. In general, he likes foods such as cooked cereals, mashed potatoes, and puddings thinner than they usually are prepared for grownups. He wants to see what he is eating, and he favors foods that are easily identified rather than mixtures of foods. His curiosity (and distrust) lead him to pull a sandwich apart or pick the different foods out of a casserole dish. Sometimes he wants each kind of food on a separate dish rather than having them touch or overlap each other on a plate.

A child needs to meet new foods, with their unfamiliar flavors, textures, temperatures, and even colors, in different ways and at different times. Some he will like the first time he meets them, especially if the feeding situation is a pleasant one. He will take longer to get acquainted with others before he enjoys them. A food dislike may last only a few days, and the child should have the opportunity to meet the food again served with different foods or prepared in a different way. There may be a few new flavors which he will never really like.

Talking about a child's food dislikes or eating problems in his presence is unwise because it gives him a reputation he may think he has to live up to! It also shows him he can annoy or worry, or perhaps bribe, his parents by the way he acts toward his food. If a child steadily refuses many foods he needs for normal growth and development, his parents need to be concerned, but they should talk to the doctor or dietitian and not show their concern to him.

A tired or unhappy or sick child is not likely to be interested in new flavors; he wants the comfort of familiar things. The same excitement of travelling and being away from home that encourages an older child to try new foods may make the young child want to revert to some of the foods he had when he was still younger.

A child may appear to be a "small eater" during the ages from about 3 to 9 years. He is growing more slowly than when he was younger and more slowly than he will when he is older. If he is eating a variety of food from the different food groups in the Daily Food Guide and if he is growing normally, his food habits are good. He should not be urged to eat more than he needs or wants. When his activity and need increase, his appetite will increase to keep pace.

SELF-REGULATION

Healthy children have a large capacity for self-regulation of the amounts of food they need. They are good judges of how much and what to eat when they have a variety of nutritious foods available and are in pleasant situations. Their judgment is not as good, however, when they can choose foods that are sweet and gooey. They are likely to eat too much of these and too little of the fruits and vegetables and milk.

One of the big responsibilities of every mother, therefore, is to see that her family has the kind of food that will make it easy for a child to judge wisely how much is right for him.

A child should never be forced to eat; he will eat what he needs when he is hungry. It is the mother's responsibility to see that he is offered simple nutritious food when he is hungry rather than foods which satisfy his appetite but contribute little in nutritive value. He should never be disciplined by being denied the food he needs for growth.

A child does not eat exactly the same amount of food every day or every week. He should be permitted to vary the amount within reasonable limits just as an adult does. Also, he goes through phases in his eating when he is tired of cooked cereal, partial to just one or two vegetables, loves peanut butter, or wants all his food mashed because he thinks chewing is too much trouble. These phases are temporary and should not create a crisis in the family.

SOME CHOICE

Developing good eating habits in a child includes having him eat the foods he needs for health and also giving him some free choice in what he eats. One reasonable way to accomplish this would be to prepare the kinds of foods that he needs and give him one small serving of every food. The servings must be small enough so he will want and need more food. This will mean second servings. Now he can have free choice of which foods he wants for seconds. Of course this same plan can apply to everyone in the family.

SNACKS

Most children eat something between meals. Preschool children, especially, need frequent refueling. A child who has become too hungry or too tired waiting for mealtime is not likely to be a good eater. Snacks should include some food from the Daily Food Guide

— milk, fruit, or bread and spread. Snacks of lone-wolf calories have no place in the young child's diet; there is no tummy space or calorie budget for them without his developing the habit of overeating.

Are some foods bad for a child? Mothers ask this particularly about highly seasoned foods, pickles, relishes, jams and jellies, and soft drinks and candy. Small firm pieces of food such as nuts, candy, raw peas, blueberries, huckleberries, whole-kernel corn are not recommended for a young child because he can choke on them. Otherwise it isn't likely that any food is harmful to a child when it is part of a well-balanced diet and when it does not give him more calories than he needs. The danger comes when specialty foods or foods chiefly with lone-wolf calories are allowed *to take the place* of foods he needs for growing. A child will not care for many of the highly seasoned foods and pickle flavors until he is older and acquires a taste for them.

A child's nutritional requirements are high in proportion to his size and his calorie need, and there is a limit to how much food he can eat or his body can use wisely. It is irresponsible of parents, therefore, to permit him to fill up on foods that do not provide the materials needed for energy and growth.

Candy often is a problem because children want too much of it or want it in place of the foods they need for growth. This is usually the result of candy being popular with the grownups, especially parents and relatives. As well as liking it themselves, they use candy as a bribe in withholding it as punishment or in giving it as a reward in many emotional situations.

In addition to candy as a competitor with other foods

which are more important for growth, there is the special problem of its effect on the teeth. Sugar on the surface and in the crevices between teeth forms an acid which attacks the tooth enamel and causes decay. Children often are given candy and other concentrated forms of sugar long before they can understand about good mouth care and about brushing their teeth.

Most of this chapter has been written about the early part of the first dozen years, and there is good reason for this. The patterns of what to do and what to think about food are formed for the child by himself and his parents during these early years of his life. These patterns will have a great influence on the child's health and food habits in the later portion of this dozen years and throughout the years that follow.

The better the early years are, then, the better the later ones are likely to be. Even if the early years have not been good, parents who are informed, understanding, and loving can achieve improvement in a child's nutrition and food habits at any age. It's never too late to begin.

14.

The Teen Years

THE TEEN YEARS may be the most eventful period of any time in your life — physically, biologically, and emotionally. The transition and growth that you experience as an adolescent can compare in importance with perhaps only one other event in your life — that of being born.

From an age standpoint you are called *teen-agers.* Perhaps it would be more accurate to call you *tweenagers.* You are not children nor quite adults. You are betwixt and between the periods of childhood dependence and adult independence — between the time when your life is controlled by adults and the time when you control it with full responsibility for yourselves as men, women, and parents.

The fitness and vigor that can come through good food and good nutrition are never more important to you than they are now. If you are a boy, your nutritional requirements will be the highest of any time in your life. If you are a girl, your requirements are higher than ever before, although they will be this high or higher when you are an expectant mother and when nursing your baby. Your food and your nutrition in these transition years will have far-reaching effects on your health in the years ahead.

You now have a great deal of control over what you eat and what you supply to your body for its growth and fitness. The job of meeting your responsibilities and enjoying your privileges will take on new meaning when you understand your food needs in relation to your progress in growth.

WHAT TO EXPECT

The Road Map of Growth tells you something of what to expect as you are becoming a young adult. To an extent you inherit a timetable for achieving your adult form with muscles and curves and length and width, so you may travel toward your adult stature faster or slower than other teen-agers. You are likely to go through stages when you seem to grow only "up" or only "out," times when your hands and feet are too big for the arms and legs they are attached to. There

ROAD MAP OF GROWTH

The ages here are from statistics. Think of yourself as an "individual," not as a "statistic." These changes may happen to you one, two, or even three years earlier or later than shown here.

When boys are 12 to 15 years and When girls are about 11 years	They start their fast-growing years
When girls are between 11 and 14 years	They are taller and heavier than boys of the same age
When boys are 14 years and When girls are 12 years	They are likely to make their greatest gains in height
When boys are about 15 and 16 years	They are now taller and heavier than girls
After boys are in their early 20's and After girls are 16	They don't grow much taller
After boys are in their early 20's and After girls are 18	They don't add much more weight, unless they add too much fat

are times when there is too much of you in some spots and not enough in others. Fortunately, these uneven stages are temporary.

Part of Nature's plan for your adult size and shape is inherited from your ancestors. This is called your body build. It is the framework on which you develop the rest of you. Whether you reach the full height possible in Nature's plan for you and whether you achieve the proportions of a fine physique and figure depend on you and your environment. In your environment food is always one of the most important items, and one about which you now can have a great deal to say.

As growth slows down, Nature turns her attention to making firmer muscles, heavier, more compact bones, and to adding substance to other tissues.

Remember, this is only a road map of growth. It is not an exact timetable.

A PHYSICAL GROWTH RECORD FOR TEEN-AGERS

As a teen-ager you probably want a standard with which you can compare your own size and growth rate. The charts on pages 147 and 148 are for this purpose. They have been made from the results of scientific studies of many boys and girls as they grew from 4 to 18 years. The figures shown are for the years from 11 to 18.

Looking at either of the charts you will see:

1. Ages are shown in 6-month intervals along the top and bottom.
2. Height is marked in inches along the right and left sides of the upper portion.
3. Weight is marked in pounds along the right and left sides of the lower portion.
4. There are 3 zones for the heights at each age from 4 to 18. These are shown in different shades and labeled Tall, Average, and Short.
5. There are 3 zones for the weights at each age. Each zone is labeled to correspond to a similar height zone and is shown in the same shading. For example, Heavy corresponds to Tall, and both are shown in the same shading. Do you see that the zones of weight are wider than the zones of height? This suggests that normally boys and girls of the same age vary more in weight than in height.

These charts are a safe guide for normal growth of boys and girls during their teen years because they allow for individual differences in body build and growth rate.

YOUR OWN GROWTH RECORD

To keep this record of your own physical growth:

1. Locate your age across the top of the appropriate chart.
2. Find your height along the left side.
3. Follow these figures toward the center until they meet.
4. Mark this point.

Now you have found your height zone. In the same way locate and mark your weight. Are you about average size? Are you taller or shorter, heavier or lighter? If your height places you in the Short Zone, then is your weight in or near the Light Zone? If your height places you in the Tall Zone, then is your weight in or near the Heavy Zone? If so, you probably have the average proportions for your size – neither quite angular nor really stocky.

The record is most useful and interesting to you if you mark your height and weight on it every three or six months. During the fast-growing years your height

The Height-Weight Charts have been prepared for the Joint Committee on Health Problems in Education of the National Education Association and American Medical Association, by Howard V. Meredith and Virginia B. Knott, University of Iowa. Individual copies of the charts are available at small cost from the order department of the American Medical Association, 535 North Dearborn Street, Chicago 10, Illinois. The charts are reproduced by courtesy of the Joint Committee.

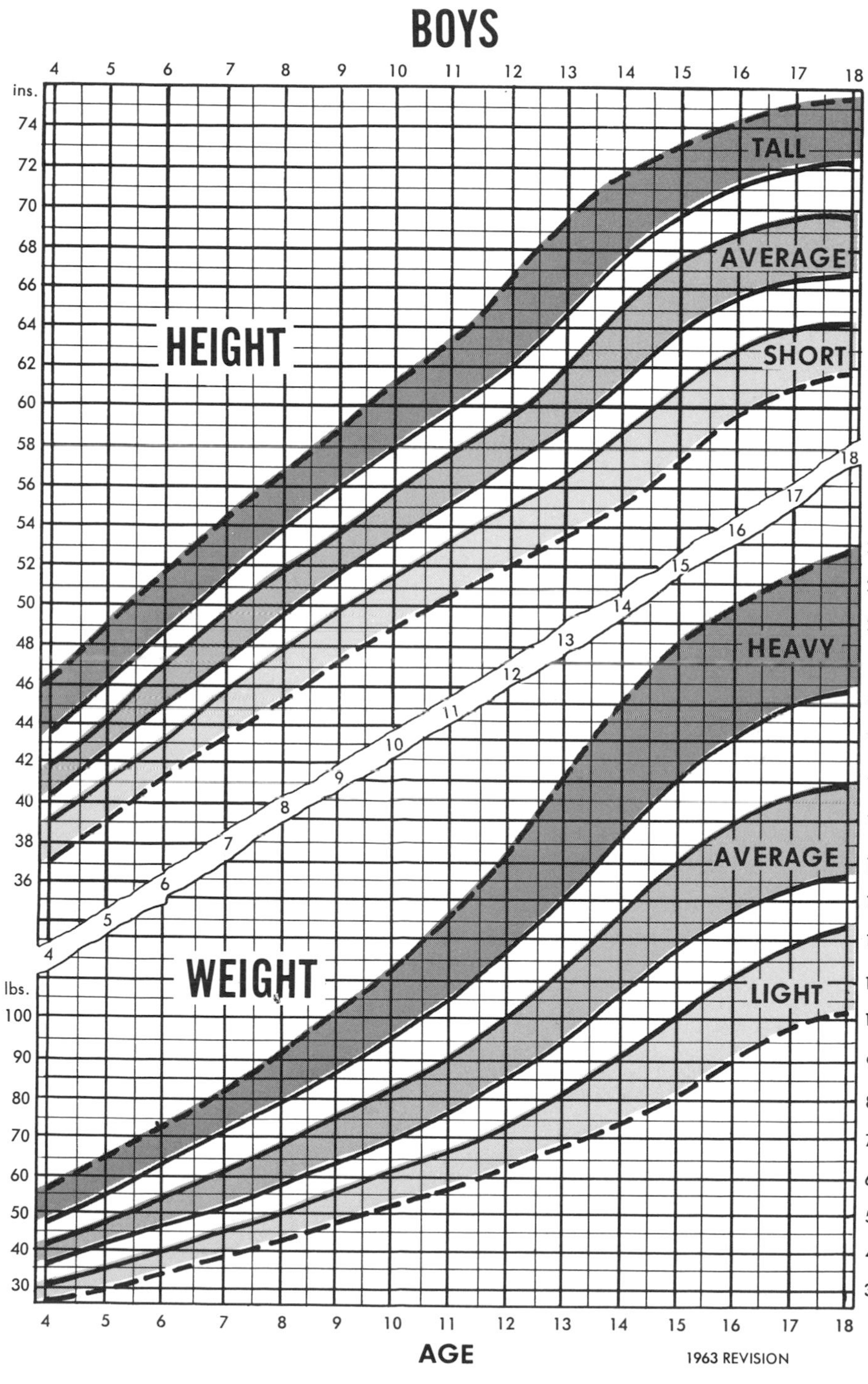

BOYS

HEIGHT

TALL

AVERAGE

SHORT

WEIGHT

HEAVY

AVERAGE

LIGHT

ins. 74 72 70 68 66 64 62 60 58 56 54 52 50 48 46 44 42 40 38 36

lbs. 220 210 200 190 180 170 160 150 140 130 120 110 100 90 80 70 60 50 40 30

AGE 4 5 6 7 8 9 10 11 12 13 14 15 16 17 18

1963 REVISION

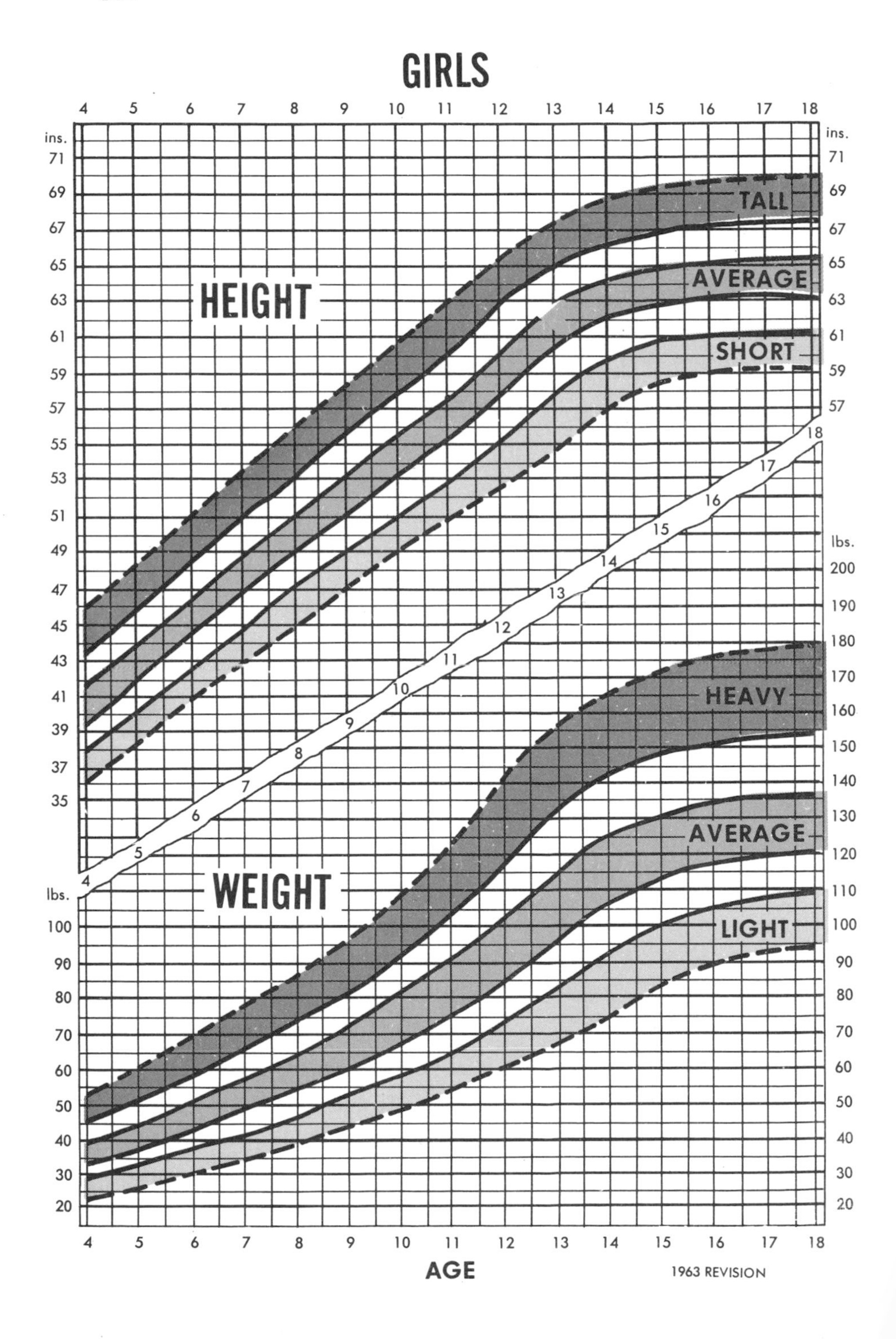
GIRLS
HEIGHT
TALL
AVERAGE
SHORT
WEIGHT
HEAVY
AVERAGE
LIGHT
ins.
lbs.
AGE
1963 REVISION

and weight may change zones. When you were 11 or 12 you may have been in the Average Zones in height and weight. Now perhaps you have grown into the Tall and Heavy Zones. Or you may be a person who grows more slowly, and you may have changed to the Short and Light Zones.

If your height and weight stay in different zones for several months or a year, you probably will want to talk to your family doctor about your record. You need his judgment as to the reason for the difference. For instance, if your height continues in the Average Zone but your weight climbs into the Heavy Zone your doctor may find that you have a heavier-than-average, or stocky, build. Then it would be only normal for your height and weight to be in slightly different zones. You are developing the proportions that suit *your framework*. This is heredity playing its part.

On the other hand, your doctor may find that you really have an average build but that you are becoming a little too heavy for *your* build. You're chubby. In that case he'll probably advise you to try to keep from gaining in weight as fast as you have been, until you grow taller. If you follow his advice, your height and weight will gradually approach corresponding zones and your proportions will improve.

Your doctor can tell you whether you are the "beanpole" type or whether you are actually underweight and need to add more weight to your framework.

The important thing is that you and your physique and figure grow to attractive proportions, whether you are short or tall, with small bones or large, until you reach the size that heredity planned for you.

NUTRIENTS AND FOOD

If you look at the Recommended Dietary Allowances on page 87, you will see that teen-age boys need much more food energy and more of every nutrient, except iron and vitamin D, than girls of the same age. They need more of many of the key nutrients when they are 15 to 18 years old and doing their fastest growing, than they did at 12 to 15 years old. The girls, however, grow their fastest when they are 12 to 15 years old, and their needs are as great or greater then than when they are 15 to 18 years old.

The Daily Food Guide makes a suitable framework for your food choices, but you must add considerably to the minimum amounts listed in order to provide enough for your growth and maturation. The Milk Group and the Vegetable-Fruit Group need special attention from you. This is not because these two food groups are more important than the other two or can replace them. It is because the Milk and Vegetable-Fruit Groups are most likely to be in short supply in the diets of teen-agers.

You now need 4 cups of milk or its equivalent each day. You need more second servings than the adults, and often the size of servings should be larger for you. You have more free choices in additional foods than the adults because your calorie budget is larger than theirs usually is.

The servings that you need every day from the four food groups have been arranged into a Basic Menu for three meals. This is a pattern you can follow in choosing the food that becomes you. The Basic Menu does not list all of the foods that you need. It is only a foundation on which you can build your total food intake for the day — a foundation for your fitness and figure.

Snacks are a popular part of your eating and social pattern. Consider them as part of your daily food supply. Be careful that you don't make them into full meals unless you can afford the calories. If you can afford the calories, be sure you include foods from your Daily Food Guide. Many foods with lone-wolf calories will satisfy your appetite without satisfying your needs for body-building materials. The girls should not be eating as much as the boys, even at parties and picnics. Sometimes they may need to skip dessert at the evening meal and save those calories for the date or party snack in the evening.

One of the disadvantages of using sweets for snacks is that the sugar which is left on and around the teeth can cause decay. If you can't always brush your teeth after eating candy or other sweet foods and beverages, learn to rinse your mouth thoroughly as soon as possible after eating them.

BASIC MENU PATTERN FOR TEEN-AGERS

This pattern is not a complete daily menu. It is an assortment of foods that will supply the major part of your needs for good nutrition. To this you can add other foods to round out your meals, or to use for snacks, and to satisfy your calorie need.

Food Group	*Number of Servings** Boy	Girl	*Example of the Kind of Food*
BREAKFAST			
Vegetable-Fruit			
A good source of vitamin C	1	1	Orange juice
Bread-Cereal	2	1	Ready-to-eat cereal Toast for the second serving
Meat	½	½	Egg—one
Milk	1	1	Milk—one cup
LUNCH OR SUPPER			
Meat	1	½	Luncheon meat
Bread-Cereal	4	2	Bread for sandwiches
Vegetable-Fruit	1	1	Cabbage slaw or apple
Milk	1	1	Milk—one cup
DINNER			
Meat	2	1	Roast beef
Vegetable-Fruit			
A good source of vitamin A	1	1	Carrots
Other	2	1	Potato
	1	1	Vegetable or fruit salad
Bread-Cereal	2	1	Rolls
Milk	1	1	Milk—one cup

Some time during the day use an additional cup of milk in some form—either milk to drink, in milk shakes, or ice cream, or in cheese or cooked foods. Also use some butter or margarine, and other fat (see Chapter 10, Fats in Food).

The servings that are listed for the boy will supply between 1,800 and 2,200 Calories, and for the girl, between 1,400 and 1,800 Calories, depending upon the particular kinds of foods chosen.

*The size of servings is given in the Daily Food Guide section, beginning on page 91.

CALORIE GUIDES

Your calorie requirement depends chiefly on your rate of growth, your activity level, and your size. Activity and size have been discussed in Chapter 4 on Activity and Calories, and here are some figures to show your calorie needs during the teen years. These figures can be helpful guides but they are not rigid rules.

Age	Calories Per Pound Per Day	
	Boys	*Girls*
12 to 15 years	31	24
15 to 18 years	26	20

Although boys 15 to 18 years need fewer calories per pound than when they were 12 to 15 years, their total daily calorie need is greater because they weigh more.

To calculate your daily calorie need, multiply the pounds you weigh by the calories suggested as your need for your age. If you are more active or have a larger body build than most teen-agers, you will need a few more calories. If you are less active or have a very small frame, you will need a few less calories. How many calories does a "few more" or a "few less" mean? Usually, about 10 per cent more or less than the averages or guides.

EXERCISE

Every normal teen-ager needs exercise — a goodly amount of it. Through exercise you train your muscles to respond readily with strength and grace to the directions you send them consciously or automatically. When the structural parts of your body work together harmoniously, the result is coordination, efficiency, and rhythm, in contrast to wasteful effort and awkwardness. Muscles, like people, need practice in learning to work together smoothly and efficiently.

You can get considerable exercise from your ordinary daily routine — especially if you walk several blocks to school or work, help around the house and yard, walk up and down a few flights of stairs, and generally take advantage of opportunities to walk or exercise.

This amount of exercise, however, is seldom enough to develop and train the muscles that help you move with ease and hold you in attractive shape. You need other regular exercise which uses all your muscles. Choosing active forms of recreation such as swimming, roller skating, dancing, and bowling is ideal.

Girls are likely to drop out of active sports when they are in the teens and confine themselves to sedentary, indoor activities. Such inactivity interferes with developing good muscle coordination, grace, strength, and stamina. It also increases the possibility of your becoming overweight, because the less active you are, the fewer calories you use and the less food energy you need.

If your situation does not seem to offer opportunity for enough activity, other than walking, consider the setting-up or daily-dozen type of exercise done in the privacy of your bedroom. These are fine because you can set your own schedule for a regular daily training period. Ask your health education teacher or your physician about exercises for your personal use. Certain exercises are particularly helpful in correcting a figure defect, such as poor posture or an awkward gait.

You are likely to need more sleep than when you were a pre-teen. Your body is working harder and faster at the job of growing a bigger and more physiologically mature *you.* Also, you are encountering many new experiences, making vital decisions, and taking serious responsibility for yourself and often for others too. Fatigue, especially when it is chronic, can interfere with your body's ability to convert food into energy and build new tissues. It also interferes with your ability to think clearly and enjoy the adventure and challenge of being a teen-ager.

Food, exercise, and sleep are among the most vital ingredients for the *you* you want to be: fine to look at, fine to know, radiating good health, interested in the world around you, and enjoying a life full of meaning and real depth.

This you can achieve. It's up to you.

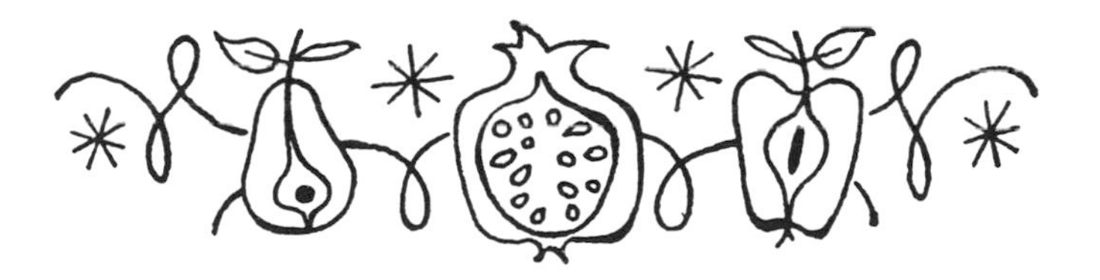

15.

Food Fads

It's a fact: As our scientific knowledge of human nutrition has increased, food fads and nutritional quackery have increased too. We have become more and more aware of the importance of food to health, of the value of knowing about the food we need, and about the composition of food we eat. Unfortunately, the quacks or charlatans have seen a chance to capitalize on our interest.

THE QUACK MAKES THE PITCH

There are several characteristics by which you can recognize a quack, charlatan, or promoter of dietary fads (he has many labels). He is almost always selling some special products — vitamin and mineral combinations, extracts or concentrates from sources not commonly used for food, or foods which he claims have been grown or prepared in such a way that they have superior and unique qualities. The cost of these to the consumer is exorbitant in relation to what it costs to produce them. In addition to wasting money, the use of such products can lead to malnutrition. Because the consumer is confident that everything he needs for good health is being supplied by the special product, he will ignore the need for eating a nutritionally adequate diet.

HE LECTURES

The promoter is often a so-called health food lecturer and writer and pretends to be a highly qualified scientist. Some of these lecturers put on a program that has all of the emotional appeal of a religious revival meeting. First he scares people about their health by claiming that the majority of persons are suffering from serious ailments which range from malnutrition to the most dreaded diseases known to man. Then he insists that by using his products and following his directions any and all the diseases will be cured. People who believe him often will delay seeing a doctor in time to prevent serious trouble.

The promoter also is extravagant and unscrupulous in making claims and promising benefits. When he quotes from scientific reports he often takes statements away from their intended meaning and distorts them to support his claims. He advertises his products in a way that appeals to people's emotions and outrages all standards of professional ethics. Often he gives a money-back guarantee.

The charlatan may operate as a door-to-door salesman. Here he takes advantage of the privacy of the home to prescribe high-priced food supplements for any disease or condition which an ailing customer may mention or which the agent may suggest.

HE ATTACKS

Despite the abundance and high quality of our American food supply, the charlatans are waging a persistent campaign to undermine the confidence of the public in the nutritional value of our foods. They have succeeded in raising serious doubts in the minds of many Americans about the integrity and purity of the nation's food supplies. It is vital to the purpose of the quacks to cast doubt on the honesty and decency of food growers and processors and the quality of the food they produce. How else can the charlatans sell their own special foods and food supplements?

These nutritional quacks also attack the U. S. Food and Drug Administration, public health officials, the American Medical Association, and nutrition authorities. They often attempt to cripple the activities of our regulatory agencies that are responsible for food inspection and standards, by questioning their authority and discrediting their work.

HE GUARANTEES

The public is spending about 100 million dollars a year for fake reducing aids that are guaranteed to take off weight. These are chiefly pills of vitamin-mineral mixture, candies of sweetened skim milk powder, and fillers or bulk. Some are harmless except to the purse, but some contain dangerous drugs. A low-calorie diet plan is enclosed with most of the products. The advertising assures you that you can lose without dieting but that you will lose faster if you follow a low calorie diet!

Do you wonder how the fake promoters can afford to give a money-back guarantee? It is because hardly ever does anyone want to admit that he has failed in getting the promised results from the product he bought. So convincing is the advertising, that the unsuccessful person decides he may have been the one at fault. He is very likely to get his money back if he asks for it, but he does not want to risk the publicity of complaining.

HE PROFITS

Distorting facts into fads and taking unscrupulous advantage of people's interest and emotions about their health is big business today. Ten million Americans are pouring 500 million dollars a year into the pockets of the promoters of dietary fads. These ten million can be hurt if they believe that the promoter's cures are a short cut to health and can take the place of good food habits and competent medical care.

OLD WIVES' TALES

There is another kind of food misinformation that can be dangerous too: the myths and superstitions which have been woven around food and handed down from one generation to another. Some of us who are horrified at the idea of following a food fad believe some of the old wives' tales about the good and bad qualities of different foods. For instance:

Milk is a food only for children, and grownups don't need it.

Milk eaten with fish or with sour fruits is harmful.

Meat is hard on the kidneys.

Fruit juices cause an acid condition in the body.

Apple cider vinegar makes the body burn fat instead of storing it.

THE WONDER OF IT

One reason for people's interest in fads and quackery and old wives' tales is the element of magic which is implied. Magic appeals to all of us; it softens the vividness of reality. To tell a person with a weight problem that she simply is eating too much — and must eat less to lose weight — is harsh reality. She would like to feel that she is a special case with a unique physical condition. In place of a low calorie diet she would prefer what seems like magic in the eat-as-usual-and-grow-thin fads.

Consider for a moment your own reactions when you go to a doctor with an ailment. Suppose he tells you that your trouble comes from excessive fatigue. He may explain that the body must have a reasonable amount of rest and relaxation in order to function normally and keep you well. He is likely to tell you also that if you persist in violating this well-established fact, little can be done to make you feel better. Do you want to be told, "Now you know what is wrong; it is up to you to get more rest?" Or would you prefer being told that yours is an unusual case, medically interesting, and requiring a special combination of drugs or food supplements beyond your comprehension — in other words, a touch of magic?

But there is more than a touch of magic in good food and good health. It is a wondrous thing how everything we are was once in our food, that the relatively simple chemical units of food can be built so accurately into the complex human body, and that the kind and amount of the food we have at every age does so much to determine our health and vigor and size. Many of us do not recognize the marvel of Nature's packages of milk, meat, eggs, grains, and fruits and vegetables, because food seems like such an ordinary everyday thing and because choosing food is a voluntary activity.

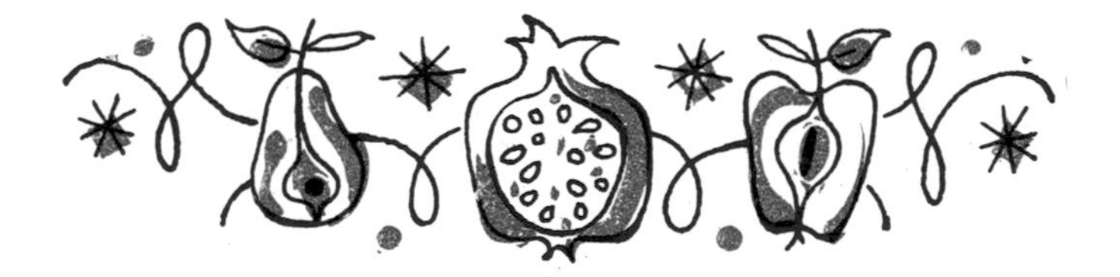

16.

What Our Money Buys

IT IS CUSTOMARY to complain about the high cost of food because we spend so much of our income for it. Actually we buy more and better food and yet spend a smaller part of our income for food than do people in any other place in the world. Wages for an hour's work here in the United States buys more food than in other countries.

Buying the food we need is investing in good nutrition, and this investment pays us continuous and generous dividends in health, well-being, satisfaction, and happiness. Of course, the amount of money we spend for food depends on how much we earn, how many persons we have to feed, and the kinds of foods we buy. The smaller our salary, the greater is the proportion of it that must go for food; and of course, the more people we have to feed, the larger our food bill. Also, we can make expensive or inexpensive choices of the foods in our Daily Food Guide and of the foods we add to the Guide.

A small amount of money spent wisely can buy better nutrition than a large amount spent carelessly. But the less money there is to spend, the more carefully we must plan, buy, and prepare food in order to have everything we need for good nutrition.

VALUES

How dull life would be if we bought food only for its nutritive value! Money spent for food buys other values too, which are not measured in terms of food energy, protein, minerals, and vitamins.

One value is the satisfaction we get from buying what we prefer — steak instead of stew meat, fresh milk instead of canned, strawberries out of season, and lots of other preferences. Fresh milk has the same nutritive value as canned evaporated milk but it costs more. The additional cost does not buy extra nutritive value but pays for the work of handling such a perishable product and keeping it available so we can buy it whenever we choose.

Another value is the security which comes with having well-stocked cupboards and refrigerators, buying ahead of our needs, and knowing we can have food whenever we want it.

Some of us buy prestige when we spend money for food. There is a prestige value to buying unusual foods, a great variety of foods, and in using these to entertain frequently and elaborately. A certain snob appeal goes with buying imported foods, having a charge account at a specialty food shop, or ordering groceries by telephone and having them delivered. The cost of these extras has nothing to do with the cost of nutritive value, but the extras are fun if we can afford them in addition to buying the foods we need for good health. We may buy social or business prestige by eating at the right places and by entertaining the right guests at the right places. It may be important to business men and women to eat lunch where other business people eat, even though they could have a better meal for less money elsewhere.

CONVENIENCE

Savings in the time and labor required to prepare foods are still other values we can buy when we spend money for food. We often call this "built-in maid service." The service may be as simple as having the tops removed from carrots or having bread cut into slices. It may be as complicated as having ready-to-heat-and-serve a complete dinner of meat, potato, and two vegetables. We can buy hundreds of items that are partially prepared and ready for us to complete or that are completely ready to serve.

We must not confuse the cost of saving time and labor with the cost of the nutritive value of our food.

When we complain that nutritious meals cost too much, we may be spending too much of our food money for *service,* and not having enough left to buy the nutritional values we need.

In using convenience foods such as meat pies or other mixtures that serve as main dishes for a meal, we should check to see if we are getting a full serving of meat or fish or whatever the main food ingredient is. Standards for the quantity of ingredients have not yet been set up for most of the commercial ready-to-serve main dishes. Convenience foods often contain more fat and carbohydrate in proportion to protein than similar items made at home. Sometimes you may think, "I couldn't make this dish any cheaper in my own kitchen." Perhaps not, but what you would make for about the same cost, or even for less cost, is likely to contain more food value and often more flavor.

How much we can afford to spend to save ourselves time and labor depends on our income and the money value of our time as well as how we prefer to spend our money for the food we need and want.

WHAT SHALL IT BE?

The problem we all face is deciding which values, in addition to the nutritive ones, we can and want to afford. Few of us can afford all of the extra values all of the time, so we choose different ones to buy at different times.

Sometimes we choose to buy built-in maid service and purchase ready-to-serve items. Another time we choose to buy food and recreation to celebrate a special occasion by eating away from home. The more money we decide to spend for the occasion, the more service, silverware, variety, and atmosphere we can buy. If we spend enough, we can buy exotic foods, entertainment, and swank galore. Other times we choose to buy a favorite food even though it is out of season or has to be brought a great distance and therefore is expensive. Whatever our choices may be, paying for them is more interesting if we recognize the different kinds of values that our money is buying.

Food is only one of the many things which our income must buy. Money for food must compete with money for housing, for clothes, for recreation, and many other things until we hardly give food a fair share of the income. We can obligate ourselves too heavily for the continuous fixed expenses such as rent, insurance, and numerous installment payments. It is not uncommon to try to save enough from the food budget to buy a new pair of shoes or a lamp, make a payment on the television set, or to buy some other item entirely unrelated to our nutrition and health. Then the food budget has to take what is left, and often this is not enough to feed us well.

Sometimes we are doing so much planning and buying for the future that we forget to provide well for today. Planning and preparing for both the near-at-hand and the far-ahead future must include day-to-day food for fitness. Good health adds meaning and pleasure to everything we do at every age. What we eat today becomes what we *are* tomorrow.

17

Table of Food Values

THE NUTRITIVE VALUES shown in the table that follows are for common household measures of food, as one cup, one ounce, or a piece of specified size. The values for some quantity that is not specified can be calculated readily. The cup measure refers to the standard 8-ounce measuring cup of 8 fluid ounces or one-half liquid pint. The ounce shown is by weight, that is, one-sixteenth of a pound avoirdupois, unless the fluid ounce is indicated.

The equivalents for most of the measures used in the food listings are:

EQUIVALENTS BY WEIGHT

1 pound (16 ounces)	= 453.6 grams
1 ounce	= 28.35 grams
3½ ounces	= 100 grams

EQUIVALENTS BY VOLUME

(All measurements level)

1 quart	= 4 cups
1 cup	= 8 fluid ounces
	= ½ pint
	= 16 tablespoons
2 tablespoons	= 1 fluid ounce
1 tablespoon	= 3 teaspoons
1 pound butter or margarine	= 4 sticks
	= 2 cups
	= 64 pats or squares
1 stick butter or margarine	= ½ cup (approximately)
	= 16 pats or squares

The nutritive values in the table apply to the parts of a food customarily eaten. They do not include the parts usually discarded, such as seeds, skins, and bone. Most of the foods listed in the table are in ready-to-serve form, but a few items frequently used as ingredients in prepared dishes have been included. Values for many of the food mixtures have been calculated from typical recipes. The cooked vegetables have no added fat.

The foods listed and the figures for their nutritive values are from "Nutritive Value of Foods," Home and Garden Bulletin No. 72, revised 1964, U.S. Department of Agriculture, Washington, D.C. 20250.

TABLE OF FOOD VALUES

[Dashes show that no basis could be found for imputing a value although there was some reason to believe that a measurable amount of the constituent might be present]

	Food, approximate measure, and weight (in grams)			Water	Food energy	Protein	Fat (total lipid)	Carbohydrate	Calcium	Iron	Vitamin A value	Thiamine	Riboflavin	Ascorbic acid
	MILK, CREAM, CHEESE; RELATED PRODUCTS		*Grams*	*Percent*	*Calories*	*Grams*	*Grams*	*Grams*	*Milligrams*	*Milligrams*	*International units*	*Milligrams*	*Milligrams*	*Milligrams*
	Milk, cow's:													
1	Fluid, whole (3.5% fat).	1 cup	244	87	160	9	9	12	288	0.1	350	0.08	0.42	2
2	Fluid, nonfat (skim)	1 cup	246	90	90	9	Trace	13	298	.1	10	.10	.44	2
3	Buttermilk, cultured, from skim milk.	1 cup	246	90	90	9	Trace	13	298	.1	10	.09	.44	2
4	Evaporated, unsweetened, undiluted.	1 cup	252	74	345	18	20	24	635	.3	820	.10	.84	3
5	Condensed, sweetened, undiluted.	1 cup	306	27	980	25	27	166	802	.3	1,090	.23	1.17	3
6	Dry, whole	1 cup	103	2	515	27	28	39	936	.5	1,160	.30	1.50	6
7	Dry, nonfat, instant	1 cup	70	3	250	25	Trace	36	905	.4	20	.24	1.25	5
	Milk, goat's:													
8	Fluid, whole	1 cup	244	88	165	8	10	11	315	.2	390	.10	.27	2
	Cream:													
9	Half-and-half (cream and milk).	1 cup	242	80	325	8	28	11	261	.1	1,160	.08	.38	2
10		1 tablespoon	15	80	20	Trace	2	1	16	Trace	70	Trace	.02	Trace
11	Light, coffee or table	1 cup	240	72	505	7	49	10	245	.1	2,030	.07	.36	2
12		1 tablespoon	15	72	30	Trace	3	1	15	Trace	130	Trace	.02	Trace
	Whipping, unwhipped (volume about double when whipped):													
13	Light	1 cup	239	62	715	6	75	9	203	.1	3,070	.06	.30	2
14		1 tablespoon	15	62	45	Trace	5	1	13	Trace	190	Trace	.02	Trace
15	Heavy	1 cup	238	57	840	5	89	7	178	.1	3,670	.05	.26	2
16		1 tablespoon	15	57	55	Trace	6	Trace	11	Trace	230	Trace	.02	Trace
	Cheese:													
17	Blue or Roquefort type	1 ounce	28	40	105	6	9	1	89	.1	350	.01	.17	0
	Cheddar or American:													
18	Ungrated	1 inch cube	17	37	70	4	5	Trace	128	.2	220	Trace	.08	0
19	Grated	1 cup	112	37	445	28	36	2	840	1.1	1,470	.03	.51	0
20		1 tablespoon	7	37	30	2	2	Trace	52	.1	90	Trace	.03	0
21	Cheddar, process	1 ounce	28	40	105	7	9	1	219	.3	350	Trace	.12	0
22	Cheese foods, Cheddar	1 ounce	28	43	90	6	7	2	162	.2	280	.01	.16	0

No.	Food, approximate measure, and weight (in grams)			Water	Food energy	Protein	Fat (total lipid)	Carbohydrate	Calcium	Iron	Vitamin A value	Thiamine	Riboflavin	scorbic acid
	MILK, CREAM, CHEESE; RELATED PRODUCTS—Continued													
	Cheese—Continued													
	Cottage cheese, from skim milk:		*Grams*	*Percent*	*Calories*	*Grams*	*Grams*	*Grams*	*Milligrams*	*Milligrams*	*International units*	*Milligrams*	*Milligrams*	*Milligrams*
23	Creamed	1 cup	225	78	240	31	9	7	212	0.7	380	0.07	0.56	0
24		1 ounce	28	78	30	4	1	1	27	.1	50	.01	.07	0
25	Uncreamed	1 cup	225	79	195	38	1	6	202	.9	20	.07	.63	0
26		1 ounce	28	79	25	5	Trace	1	26	.1	Trace	.01	.08	0
27	Cream cheese	1 ounce	28	51	105	2	11	1	18	.1	440	Trace	.07	0
28		1 tablespoon	15	51	55	1	6	Trace	9	Trace	230	Trace	.04	0
29	Swiss (domestic)	1 ounce	28	39	105	8	8	1	262	.3	320	Trace	.11	0
	Milk beverages:													
30	Cocoa	1 cup	242	79	235	9	11	26	286	.9	390	.09	.45	2
31	Chocolate-flavored milk drink (made with skim milk).	1 cup	250	83	190	8	6	27	270	.4	210	.09	.41	2
32	Malted milk	1 cup	270	78	280	13	12	32	364	.8	670	.17	.56	2
	Milk desserts:													
33	Cornstarch pudding, plain (blanc mange).	1 cup	248	76	275	9	10	39	290	.1	390	.07	.40	2
34	Custard, baked	1 cup	248	77	285	13	14	28	278	1.0	870	.10	.47	1
	Ice cream, plain, factory packed:													
35	Slice or cut brick, ⅛ of quart brick.	1 slice or cut brick.	71	62	145	3	9	15	87	.1	370	.03	.13	1
36	Container	3½ fluid ounces.	62	62	130	2	8	13	76	.1	320	.03	.12	1
37	Container	8 fluid ounces.	142	62	295	6	18	29	175	.1	740	.06	.27	1
38	Ice milk	1 cup	187	67	285	9	10	42	292	.2	390	.09	.41	2
39	Yoghurt, from partially skimmed milk.	1 cup	246	89	120	8	4	13	295	.1	170	.09	.43	2
	EGGS													
	Eggs, large, 24 ounces per dozen:													
	Raw:													
40	Whole, without shell	1 egg	50	/4	80	6	6	Trace	27	1.1	590	.05	.15	0

No.	Food	Measure	Weight											
41	White of egg	1 white	33	88	15	4	Trace	Trace	3	Trace	0	Trace	.09	0
42	Yolk of egg	1 yolk	17	51	60	3	5	Trace	24	.9	580	.04	.07	0
	Cooked:													
43	Boiled, shell removed	2 eggs	100	74	160	13	12	1	54	2.3	1,180	.09	.28	0
44	Scrambled, with milk and fat.	1 egg	64	72	110	7	8	1	51	1.1	690	.05	.18	0
	MEAT, POULTRY, FISH, SHELLFISH; RELATED PRODUCTS													
45	Bacon, broiled or fried, crisp.	2 slices	16	8	100	5	8	1	2	.5	0	.08	.05	------
	Beef, trimmed to retail basis,[1] cooked:													
	Cuts braised, simmered, or pot-roasted:													
46	Lean and fat	3 ounces	85	53	245	23	16	0	10	2.9	30	.04	.18	------
47	Lean only	2.5 ounces	72	62	140	22	5	0	10	2.7	10	.04	.16	------
	Hamburger (ground beef), broiled:													
48	Lean	3 ounces	85	60	185	23	10	0	10	3.0	20	.08	.20	------
49	Regular	3 ounces	85	54	245	21	17	0	9	2.7	30	.07	.18	------
	Roast, oven-cooked, no liquid added:													
	Relatively fat, such as rib:													
50	Lean and fat	3 ounces	85	40	375	17	34	0	8	2.2	70	.05	.13	------
51	Lean only	1.8 ounces	51	57	125	14	7	0	6	1.8	10	.04	.11	------
	Relatively lean, such as heel of round:													
52	Lean and fat	3 ounces	85	62	165	25	7	0	11	3.2	10	.06	.19	------
53	Lean only	2.7 ounces	78	65	125	24	3	0	10	3.0	Trace	.06	.18	------
	Steak, broiled:													
	Relatively fat, such as sirloin:													
54	Lean and fat	3 ounces	85	44	330	20	27	0	9	2.5	50	.05	.16	------
55	Lean only	2.0 ounces	56	59	115	18	4	0	7	2.2	10	.05	.14	------
	Relatively lean, such as round:													
56	Lean and fat	3 ounces	85	55	220	24	13	0	10	3.0	20	.07	.19	------
57	Lean only	2.4 ounces	68	61	130	21	4	0	9	2.5	10	.06	.16	------
	Beef, canned:													
58	Corned beef	3 ounces	85	59	185	22	10	0	17	3.7	20	.01	.20	------
59	Corned beef hash	3 ounces	85	67	155	7	10	9	11	1.7	------	.01	.08	------
60	Beef, dried or chipped	2 ounces	57	48	115	19	4	0	11	2.9	------	.04	.18	------
61	Beef and vegetable stew	1 cup	235	82	210	15	10	15	28	2.8	2,310	.13	.17	15
62	Beef potpie, baked: Individual pie, 4¼-inch diameter, weight before baking about 8 ounces.	1 pie	227	55	560	23	33	43	32	4.1	1,860	.25	.27	7

[1] Outer layer of fat on the cut was removed to within approximately ½ inch of the lean. Deposits of fat within the cut were not removed.

	Food, approximate measure, and weight (in grams)			Water	Food energy	Protein	Fat (total lipid)	Carbohydrate	Calcium	Iron	Vitamin A value	Thiamine	Riboflavin	Ascorbic acid
	MEAT, POULTRY, FISH, SHELLFISH; RELATED PRODUCTS—Continued													
	Chicken, cooked:		*Grams*	*Percent*	*Calories*	*Grams*	*Grams*	*Grams*	*Milligrams*	*Milligrams*	*International units*	*Milligrams*	*Milligrams*	*Milligrams*
63	Flesh only, broiled	3 ounces	85	71	115	20	3	0	8	1.4	80	0.05	0.16	------
	Breast, fried, ½ breast:													
64	With bone	3.3 ounces	94	58	155	25	5	1	9	1.3	70	.04	.17	------
65	Flesh and skin only	2.7 ounces	76	58	155	25	5	1	9	1.3	70	.04	.17	------
	Drumstick, fried:													
66	With bone	2.1 ounces	59	55	90	12	4	Trace	6	.9	50	.03	.15	------
67	Flesh and skin only	1.3 ounces	38	55	90	12	4	Trace	6	.9	50	.03	.15	------
68	Chicken, canned, boneless	3 ounces	85	65	170	18	10	0	18	1.3	200	.03	.11	3
	Chicken potpie. *See* Poultry potpie.													
	Chile con carne, canned:													
69	With beans	1 cup	250	72	335	19	15	30	80	4.2	150	.08	.18	------
70	Without beans	1 cup	255	67	510	26	38	15	97	3.6	380	.05	.31	------
71	Heart, beef, lean, braised	3 ounces	85	61	160	27	5	1	5	5.0	20	.21	1.04	1
	Lamb, trimmed to retail basis,[1] cooked:													
72	Chop, thick, with bone, broiled.	1 chop, 4.8 ounces.	137	47	400	25	33	0	10	1.5	------	.14	.25	------
73	Lean and fat	4.0 ounces	112	47	400	25	33	0	10	1.5	------	.14	.25	------
74	Lean only	2.6 ounces	74	62	140	21	6	0	9	1.5	------	.11	.20	------
	Leg, roasted:													
75	Lean and fat	3 ounces	85	54	235	22	16	0	9	1.4	------	.13	.23	------
76	Lean only	2.5 ounces	71	62	130	20	5	0	9	1.4	------	.12	.21	------
	Shoulder, roasted:													
77	Lean and fat	3 ounces	85	50	285	18	23	0	9	1.0	------	.11	.20	------
78	Lean only	2.3 ounces	64	61	130	17	6	0	8	1.0	------	.10	.18	------
79	Liver, beef, fried	2 ounces	57	57	130	15	6	3	6	5.0	30,280	.15	2.37	15
	Pork, cured, cooked:													
80	Ham, light cure, lean and fat, roasted.	3 ounces	85	54	245	18	19	0	8	2.2	0	.40	.16	------

81	Luncheon meat:													
82	Boiled ham, sliced	2 ounces	57	59	135	11	10	0	6	1.6	0	.25	.09	------
	Canned, spiced or unspiced.	2 ounces	57	55	165	8	14	1	5	1.2	0	.18	.12	------
83	Pork, fresh, trimmed to retail basis,[1] cooked:													
	Chop, thick, with bone	1 chop, 3.5 ounces.	98	42	260	16	21	0	8	2.2	0	.63	.18	------
84														
85	Lean and fat	2.3 ounces	66	42	260	16	21	0	8	2.2	0	.63	.18	------
	Lean only	1.7 ounces	48	53	130	15	7	0	7	1.9	0	.54	.16	------
86	Roast, oven-cooked, no liquid added:													
87	Lean and fat	3 ounces	85	46	310	21	24	0	9	2.7	0	.78	.22	------
	Lean only	2.4 ounces	68	55	175	20	10	0	9	2.6	0	.73	.21	------
88	Cuts, simmered:													
89	Lean and fat	3 ounces	85	46	320	20	26	0	8	2.5	0	.46	.21	------
90	Lean only	2.2 ounces	63	60	135	18	6	0	8	2.3	0	.42	.19	------
	Poultry potpie (based on chicken potpie). Individual pie, 4¼-inch diameter, weight before baking about 8 ounces.	1 pie	227	57	535	23	31	42	68	3.0	3,020	.25	.26	5
91	Sausage:													
	Bologna, slice, 4.1 by 0.1 inch.	8 slices	227	56	690	27	62	2	16	4.1	------	.36	.49	------
92														
93	Frankfurter, cooked	1 frankfurter	51	58	155	6	14	1	3	.8	------	.08	.10	------
	Pork, links or patty, cooked.	4 ounces	113	35	540	21	50	Trace	8	2.7	0	.89	.39	------
94														
	Tongue, beef, braised	3 ounces	85	61	210	18	14	Trace	6	1.9	------	.04	.25	------
	Turkey potpie. *See* Poultry potpie.													
95	Veal, cooked:													
	Cutlet, without bone, broiled.	3 ounces	85	60	185	23	9	------	9	2.7	------	.06	.21	------
96	Roast, medium fat, medium done; lean and fat.	3 ounces	85	55	230	23	14	0	10	2.9	------	.11	.26	------
	Fish and shellfish:													
97	Bluefish, baked or broiled.	3 ounces	85	68	135	22	4	0	25	.6	40	.09	.08	------
	Clams:													
98	Raw, meat only	3 ounces	85	82	65	11	1	2	59	5.2	90	.08	.15	8
99	Canned, solids and liquid.	3 ounces	85	86	45	7	1	2	47	3.5	------	.01	.09	------
100	Crabmeat, canned	3 ounces	85	77	85	15	2	1	38	.7	------	.07	.07	------
101	Fish sticks, breaded, cooked, frozen; stick, 3.8 by 1.0 by 0.5 inch.	10 sticks or 8-ounce package.	227	66	400	38	20	15	25	.9	------	.09	.16	------

[1] Outer layer of fat on the cut was removed to within approximately ½ inch of the lean. Deposits of fat within the cut were not removed.

No.	Food, approximate measure, and weight (in grams)			Water	Food energy	Protein	Fat (total lipid)	Carbohydrate	Calcium	Iron	Vitamin A value	Thiamine	Riboflavin	Ascorbic acid
	MEAT, POULTRY, FISH, SHELLFISH; RELATED PRODUCTS—Continued													
	Fish and shellfish—Continued		*Grams*	*Percent*	*Calories*	*Grams*	*Grams*	*Grams*	*Milligrams*	*Milligrams*	*International units*	*Milligrams*	*Milligrams*	*Milligrams*
102	Haddock, fried	3 ounces	85	66	140	17	5	5	34	1.0	-------	0.03	0.06	2
	Mackerel:													
103	Broiled, Atlantic	3 ounces	85	62	200	19	13	0	5	1.0	450	.13	.23	------
104	Canned, Pacific, solids and liquid.[2]	3 ounces	85	66	155	18	9	0	221	1.9	20	.02	.28	------
105	Ocean perch, breaded (egg and breadcrumbs), fried.	3 ounces	85	59	195	16	11	6	28	1.1	-------	.08	.09	------
106	Oysters, meat only: Raw, 13–19 medium selects.	1 cup	240	85	160	20	4	8	226	13.2	740	.33	.43	------
107	Oyster stew, 1 part oysters to 3 parts milk by volume, 3–4 oysters.	1 cup	230	84	200	11	12	11	269	3.3	640	.13	.41	------
108	Salmon, pink, canned	3 ounces	85	71	120	17	5	0	[3] 167	.7	60	.03	.16	------
109	Sardines, Atlantic, canned in oil, drained solids.	3 ounces	85	62	175	20	9	0	372	2.5	190	.02	.17	------
110	Shad, baked	3 ounces	85	64	170	20	10	0	20	.5	20	.11	.22	------
111	Shrimp, canned, meat only.	3 ounces	85	70	100	21	1	1	98	2.6	50	.01	.03	------
112	Swordfish, broiled with butter or margarine.	3 ounces	85	65	150	24	5	0	23	1.1	1,750	.03	.04	------
113	Tuna, canned in oil, drained solids.	3 ounces	85	61	170	24	7	0	7	1.6	70	.04	.10	------
	MATURE DRY BEANS AND PEAS, NUTS, PEANUTS; RELATED PRODUCTS													
114	Almonds, shelled	1 cup	142	5	850	26	77	28	332	6.7	0	.34	1.31	Trace

	Beans, dry:													
	Common varieties, such as Great Northern, navy, and others, canned:													
115	Red	1 cup	256	76	230	15	1	42	74	4.6	Trace	.13	.10	------
	White, with tomato sauce:													
116	With pork	1 cup	261	71	320	16	7	50	141	4.7	340	.20	.08	5
117	Without pork	1 cup	261	68	310	16	1	60	177	5.2	160	.18	.09	5
118	Lima, cooked	1 cup	192	64	260	16	1	48	56	5.6	Trace	.26	.12	Trace
119	Brazil nuts	1 cup	140	5	915	20	94	15	260	4.8	Trace	1.34	.17	------
120	Cashew nuts, roasted	1 cup	135	5	760	23	62	40	51	5.1	140	.58	.33	------
	Coconut:													
121	Fresh, shredded	1 cup	97	51	335	3	34	9	13	1.6	0	.05	.02	3
122	Dried, shredded, sweetened.	1 cup	62	3	340	2	24	33	10	1.2	0	.02	.02	0
123	Cowpeas or blackeye peas, dry, cooked.	1 cup	248	80	190	13	1	34	42	3.2	20	.41	.11	Trace
	Peanuts, roasted, salted:													
124	Halves	1 cup	144	2	840	37	72	27	107	3.0	-------	.46	.19	0
125	Chopped	1 tablespoon	9	2	55	2	4	2	7	.2	-------	.03	.01	0
126	Peanut butter	1 tablespoon	16	2	95	4	8	3	9	.3	-------	.02	.02	0
127	Peas, split, dry, cooked	1 cup	250	70	290	20	1	52	28	4.2	100	.37	.22	------
	Pecans:													
128	Halves	1 cup	108	3	740	10	77	16	79	2.6	140	.93	.14	2
129	Chopped	1 tablespoon	7.5	3	50	1	5	1	5	.2	10	.06	.01	Trace
	Walnuts, shelled:													
130	Black or native, chopped.	1 cup	126	3	790	26	75	19	Trace	7.6	380	.28	.14	------
	English or Persian:													
131	Halves	1 cup	100	4	650	15	64	16	99	3.1	30	.33	.13	3
132	Chopped	1 tablespoon	8	4	50	1	5	1	8	.2	Trace	.03	.01	Trace
	VEGETABLES AND VEGETABLE PRODUCTS													
	Asparagus:													
133	Cooked, cut spears	1 cup	175	94	35	4	Trace	6	37	1.0	1,580	.27	.32	46
	Canned spears, medium:													
134	Green	6 spears	96	92	20	2	Trace	3	18	1.8	770	.06	.10	14
135	Bleached	6 spears	96	92	20	2	Trace	4	15	1.0	80	.05	.06	14
	Beans:													
136	Lima, immature, cooked	1 cup	160	71	180	12	1	32	75	4.0	450	.29	.16	28
	Snap, green:													
	Cooked:													
137	In small amount of water, short time.	1 cup	125	92	30	2	Trace	7	62	.8	680	.08	.11	16

[2] Vitamin values based on drained solids.

[3] Based on total contents of can. If bones are discarded, value will be greatly reduced.

No.	Food, approximate measure, and weight (in grams)			Water	Food energy	Protein	Fat (total lipid)	Carbohydrate	Calcium	Iron	Vitamin A value	Thiamine	Riboflavin	Ascorbic acid
	VEGETABLES AND VEGETABLE PRODUCTS—Continued													
	Beans—Continued													
	Snap, green—Continued													
	Cooked—Continued		*Grams*	*Per-cent*	*Calo-ries*	*Grams*	*Grams*	*Grams*	*Milli-grams*	*Milli-grams*	*Inter-national units*	*Milli-grams*	*Milli-grams*	*Milli-grams*
138	In large amount of water, long time.	1 cup	125	92	30	2	Trace	7	62	0.8	680	0.07	0.10	13
	Canned:													
139	Solids and liquid	1 cup	239	94	45	2	Trace	10	81	2.9	690	.08	.10	9
140	Strained or chopped (baby food).	1 ounce	28	92	5	Trace	Trace	1	9	.3	110	.01	.02	Trace
	Bean sprouts. *See* Sprouts.													
141	Beets, cooked, diced	1 cup	165	91	50	2	Trace	12	23	.8	40	.04	.07	11
142	Broccoli spears, cooked	1 cup	150	91	40	5	Trace	7	132	1.2	3,750	.14	.29	135
143	Brussels sprouts, cooked	1 cup	130	88	45	5	1	8	42	1.4	680	.10	.18	113
	Cabbage:													
	Raw:													
144	Finely shredded	1 cup	100	92	25	1	Trace	5	49	.4	130	.05	.05	47
145	Coleslaw	1 cup	120	83	120	1	9	9	52	.5	180	.06	.06	35
	Cooked:													
146	In small amount of water, short time.	1 cup	170	94	35	2	Trace	7	75	.5	220	.07	.07	56
147	In large amount of water, long time.	1 cup	170	94	30	2	Trace	7	71	.5	200	.04	.04	40
	Cabbage, celery or Chinese:													
148	Raw, leaves and stalk, 1-inch pieces.	1 cup	100	95	15	1	Trace	3	43	.6	150	.05	.04	25
149	Cabbage, spoon (or pakchoy), cooked.	1 cup	150	95	20	2	Trace	4	222	.9	4,650	.07	.12	23
	Carrots:													
	Raw:													
150	Whole, 5½ by 1 inch, (25 thin strips).	1 carrot	50	88	20	1	Trace	5	18	.4	5,500	.03	.03	4
151	Grated	1 cup	110	88	45	1	Trace	11	41	.8	12,100	.06	.06	9

152	Cooked, diced	1 cup	145	91	45	1	Trace	10	48	.9	15,220	.08	.07	9
153	Canned, strained or chopped (baby food).	1 ounce	28	92	10	Trace	Trace	2	7	.1	3,690	.01	.01	1
154	Cauliflower, cooked, flowerbuds.	1 cup	120	93	25	3	Trace	5	25	.8	70	.11	.10	66
	Celery, raw:													
155	Stalk, large outer, 8 by about 1½ inches, at root end.	1 stalk	40	94	5	Trace	Trace	2	16	.1	100	.01	.01	4
156	Pieces, diced	1 cup	100	94	15	1	Trace	4	39	.3	240	.03	.03	9
157	Collards, cooked	1 cup	190	91	55	5	1	9	289	1.1	10,260	.27	.37	87
	Corn, sweet:													
158	Cooked, ear 5 by 1¾ inches.[4]	1 ear	140	74	70	3	1	16	2	.5	[5] 310	.09	.08	7
159	Canned, solids and liquid.	1 cup	256	81	170	5	2	40	10	1.0	[5] 690	.07	.12	13
160	Cowpeas, cooked, immature seeds.	1 cup	160	72	175	13	1	29	38	3.4	560	.49	.18	28
	Cucumbers, 10-ounce; 7½ by about 2 inches:													
161	Raw, pared	1 cucumber	207	96	30	1	Trace	7	35	.6	Trace	.07	.09	23
162	Raw, pared, center slice ⅛-inch thick.	6 slices	50	96	5	Trace	Trace	2	8	.2	Trace	.02	.02	6
163	Dandelion greens, cooked.	1 cup	180	90	60	4	1	12	252	3.2	21,060	.24	.29	32
164	Endive, curly (including escarole).	2 ounces	57	93	10	1	Trace	2	46	1.0	1,870	.04	.08	6
165	Kale, leaves including stems, cooked.	1 cup	110	91	30	4	1	4	147	1.3	8,140	-------	-------	68
	Lettuce, raw:													
166	Butterhead, as Boston types; head, 4-inch diameter.	1 head	220	95	30	3	Trace	6	77	4.4	2,130	.14	.13	18
167	Crisphead, as Iceberg; head, 4¾-inch diameter.	1 head	454	96	60	4	Trace	13	91	2.3	1,500	.29	.27	29
168	Looseleaf, or bunching varieties, leaves.	2 large	50	94	10	1	Trace	2	34	.7	950	.03	.04	9
169	Mushrooms, canned, solids and liquid.	1 cup	244	93	40	5	Trace	6	15	1.2	Trace	.04	.60	4
170	Mustard greens, cooked	1 cup	140	93	35	3	1	6	193	2.5	8,120	.11	.19	68
171	Okra, cooked, pod 3 by ⅝ inch.	8 pods	85	91	25	2	Trace	5	78	.4	420	.11	.15	17

[4] Measure and weight apply to entire vegetable or fruit including parts not usually eaten.

[5] Based on yellow varieties; white varieties contain only a trace of cryptoxanthin and carotenes, the pigments in corn that have biological activity.

	Food, approximate measure, and weight (in grams)			Water	Food energy	Protein	Fat (total lipid)	Carbohydrate	Calcium	Iron	Vitamin A value	Thiamine	Riboflavin	Ascorbic acid
	VEGETABLES AND VEGETABLE PRODUCTS—Continued													
	Onions:													
	Mature:		*Grams*	*Percent*	*Calories*	*Grams*	*Grams*	*Grams*	*Milligrams*	*Milligrams*	*International units*	*Milligrams*	*Milligrams*	*Milligrams*
172	Raw, onion 2½-inch diameter.	1 onion	110	89	40	2	Trace	10	30	0.6	40	0.04	0.04	11
173	Cooked	1 cup	210	92	60	3	Trace	14	50	.8	80	.06	.06	14
174	Young green, small, without tops.	6 onions	50	88	20	1	Trace	5	20	.3	Trace	.02	.02	12
175	Parsley, raw, chopped	1 tablespoon	3.5	85	1	Trace	Trace	Trace	7	.2	300	Trace	.01	6
176	Parsnips, cooked	1 cup	155	82	100	2	1	23	70	.9	50	.11	.13	16
	Peas, green:													
177	Cooked	1 cup	160	82	115	9	1	19	37	2.9	860	.44	.17	33
178	Canned, solids and liquid.	1 cup	249	83	165	9	1	31	50	4.2	1,120	.23	.13	22
179	Canned, strained (baby food).	1 ounce	28	86	15	1	Trace	3	3	.4	140	.02	.02	3
180	Peppers, hot, red, without seeds, dried (ground chili powder, added seasonings).	1 tablespoon	15	8	50	2	2	8	40	2.3	9,750	.03	.17	2
	Peppers, sweet:													
	Raw, medium, about 6 per pound:													
181	Green pod without stem and seeds.	1 pod	62	93	15	1	Trace	3	6	.4	260	.05	.05	79
182	Red pod without stem and seeds.	1 pod	60	91	20	1	Trace	4	8	.4	2,670	.05	.05	122
183	Canned, pimientos, medium.	1 pod	38	92	10	Trace	Trace	2	3	.6	870	.01	.02	36

	Potatoes, medium (about 3 per pound raw):													
184	Baked, peeled after baking.	1 potato	99	75	90	3	Trace	21	9	.7	Trace	.10	.04	20
	Boiled:													
185	Peeled after boiling	1 potato	136	80	105	3	Trace	23	10	.8	Trace	.13	.05	22
186	Peeled before boiling	1 potato	122	83	80	2	Trace	18	7	.6	Trace	.11	.04	20
	French-fried, piece 2 by ½ by ½ inch:													
187	Cooked in deep fat	10 pieces	57	45	155	2	7	20	9	.7	Trace	.07	.04	12
188	Frozen, heated	10 pieces	57	53	125	2	5	19	5	1.0	Trace	.08	.01	12
	Mashed:													
189	Milk added	1 cup	195	83	125	4	1	25	47	.8	50	.16	.10	19
190	Milk and butter added.	1 cup	195	80	185	4	8	24	47	.8	330	.16	.10	18
191	Potato chips, medium, 2-inch diameter.	10 chips	20	2	115	1	8	10	8	.4	Trace	.04	.01	3
192	Pumpkin, canned	1 cup	228	90	75	2	1	18	57	.9	14, 590	.07	.12	12
193	Radishes, raw, small, without tops.	4 radishes	40	94	5	Trace	Trace	1	12	.4	Trace	.01	.01	10
194	Sauerkraut, canned, solids and liquid.	1 cup	235	93	45	2	Trace	9	85	1.2	120	.07	.09	33
	Spinach:													
195	Cooked	1 cup	180	92	40	5	1	6	167	4.0	14, 580	.13	.25	50
196	Canned, drained solids	1 cup	180	91	45	5	1	6	212	4.7	14, 400	.03	.21	24
197	Canned, strained or chopped (baby food).	1 ounce	28	88	10	1	Trace	2	18	.2	1, 420	.01	.04	2
	Sprouts, raw:													
198	Mung bean	1 cup	90	89	30	3	Trace	6	17	1.2	20	.12	.12	17
199	Soybean	1 cup	107	89	40	6	2	4	46	.7	90	.17	.16	4
	Squash:													
	Cooked:													
200	Summer, diced	1 cup	210	96	30	2	Trace	7	52	.8	820	.10	.16	21
201	Winter, baked, mashed.	1 cup	205	81	130	4	1	32	57	1.6	8, 610	.10	.27	27
202	Canned, winter, strained and chopped (baby food).	1 ounce	28	92	10	Trace	Trace	2	7	.1	510	.01	.01	1

	Food, approximate measure, and weight (in grams)			Water	Food energy	Protein	Fat (total lipid)	Carbohydrate	Calcium	Iron	Vitamin A value	Thiamine	Riboflavin	Ascorbic acid
	VEGETABLES AND VEGETABLE PRODUCTS—Continued													
	Sweetpotatoes:													
	Cooked, medium, 5 by 2 inches, weight raw about 6 ounces:		*Grams*	*Percent*	*Calories*	*Grams*	*Grams*	*Grams*	*Milligrams*	*Milligrams*	*International units*	*Milligrams*	*Milligrams*	*Milligrams*
203	Baked, peeled after baking.	1 sweetpotato.	110	64	155	2	1	36	44	1.0	8,910	0.10	0.07	24
204	Boiled, peeled after boiling.	1 sweetpotato.	147	71	170	2	1	39	47	1.0	11,610	.13	.09	25
205	Candied, 3½ by 2¼ inches.	1 sweetpotato.	175	60	295	2	6	60	65	1.6	11,030	.10	.08	17
206	Canned, vacuum or solid pack.	1 cup	218	72	235	4	Trace	54	54	1.7	17,000	.10	.10	30
	Tomatoes:													
207	Raw, medium, 2 by 2½ inches, about 3 per pound.	1 tomato	150	94	35	2	Trace	7	20	.8	1,350	.10	.06	[6] 34
208	Canned	1 cup	242	94	50	2	Trace	10	15	1.2	2,180	.13	.07	40
209	Tomato juice, canned	1 cup	242	94	45	2	Trace	10	17	2.2	1,940	.13	.07	39
210	Tomato catsup	1 tablespoon	17	69	15	Trace	Trace	4	4	.1	240	.02	.01	3
211	Turnips, cooked, diced	1 cup	155	94	35	1	Trace	8	54	.6	Trace	.06	.08	33
	Turnip greens:													
	Cooked:													
212	In small amount of water, short time.	1 cup	145	93	30	3	Trace	5	267	1.6	9,140	.21	.36	100
213	In large amount of water, long time.	1 cup	145	94	25	3	Trace	5	252	1.4	8,260	.14	.33	68
214	Canned, solids and liquid	1 cup	232	94	40	3	1	7	232	3.7	10,900	.04	.21	44
	FRUITS AND FRUIT PRODUCTS													
215	Apples, raw, medium, 2½-inch diameter, about 3 per pound.[4]	1 apple	150	85	70	Trace	Trace	18	8	.4	50	.04	.02	3
216	Apple brown betty	1 cup	230	64	345	4	8	68	41	1.4	230	.13	.10	3

217	Apple juice, bottled or canned.	1 cup	249	88	120	Trace	Trace	30	15	1.5	-------	.01	.04	2
	Applesauce, canned:													
218	Sweetened	1 cup	254	76	230	1	Trace	60	10	1.3	100	.05	.03	3
219	Unsweetened or artificially sweetened.	1 cup	239	88	100	Trace	Trace	26	10	1.2	100	.04	.02	2
220	Applesauce and apricots, canned, strained or junior (baby food).	1 ounce	28	77	25	Trace	Trace	6	1	.1	170	Trace	Trace	1
	Apricots:													
221	Raw, about 12 per pound.[4]	3 apricots	114	85	55	1	Trace	14	18	.5	2,890	.03	.04	10
	Canned in heavy sirup:													
222	Halves and sirup	1 cup	259	77	220	2	Trace	57	28	.8	4,510	.05	.06	10
223	Halves (medium) and sirup.	4 halves; 2 tablespoons sirup.	122	77	105	1	Trace	27	13	.4	2,120	.02	.03	5
	Dried:													
224	Uncooked, 40 halves, small.	1 cup	150	25	390	8	1	100	100	8.2	16,350	.02	.23	19
225	Cooked, unsweetened, fruit and liquid.	1 cup	285	76	240	5	1	62	63	5.1	8,550	.01	.13	8
226	Apricot nectar, canned	1 cup	250	85	140	1	Trace	36	22	.5	2,380	.02	.02	7
	Avocados, raw:													
	California varieties, mainly Fuerte:													
227	10-ounce avocado, about 3⅓ by 4¼ inches, peeled, pitted.	½ avocado	108	74	185	2	18	6	11	.6	310	.12	.21	15
228	½-inch cubes	1 cup	152	74	260	3	26	9	15	.9	440	.16	.30	21
	Florida varieties:													
229	13-ounce avocado, about 4 by 3 inches, peeled, pitted.	½ avocado	123	78	160	2	14	11	12	.7	360	.13	.24	17
230	½-inch cubes	1 cup	152	78	195	2	17	13	15	.9	440	.16	.30	21
231	Bananas, raw, 6 by 1½ inches, about 3 per pound.[4]	1 banana	150	76	85	1	Trace	23	8	.7	190	.05	.06	10
232	Blackberries, raw	1 cup	144	84	85	2	1	19	46	1.3	290	.05	.06	30
233	Blueberries, raw	1 cup	140	83	85	1	1	21	21	1.4	140	.04	.08	20
234	Cantaloups, raw; medium, 5-inch diameter, about 1⅔ pounds.[4]	½ melon	385	91	60	1	Trace	14	27	.8	[7]6,540	.08	.06	63

[4] Measure and weight apply to entire vegetable or fruit including parts not usually eaten.

[6] Year-round average. Samples marketed from November through May average around 15 milligrams per 150-gram tomato; from June through October, around 39 milligrams.

[7] Value based on varieties with orange-colored flesh, for green-fleshed varieties value is about 540 I.U. per ½ melon.

No.	Food, approximate measure, and weight (in grams)	Measure	Weight	Water	Food energy	Protein	Fat (total lipid)	Carbohydrate	Calcium	Iron	Vitamin A value	Thiamine	Riboflavin	Ascorbic acid
	FRUITS AND FRUIT PRODUCTS—Con.													
	Cherries:		*Grams*	*Percent*	*Calories*	*Grams*	*Grams*	*Grams*	*Milligrams*	*Milligrams*	*International units*	*Milligrams*	*Milligrams*	*Milligrams*
235	Raw, sweet, with stems [4]	1 cup	130	80	80	2	Trace	20	26	0.5	130	0.06	0.07	12
236	Canned, red, sour, pitted, heavy sirup.	1 cup	260	76	230	2	1	59	36	.8	1,680	.07	.06	13
237	Cranberry juice cocktail, canned.	1 cup	250	83	160	Trace	Trace	41	12	.8	Trace	.02	.02	(8)
238	Cranberry sauce, sweetened, canned, strained.	1 cup	277	62	405	Trace	1	104	17	.6	40	.03	.03	5
239	Dates, domestic, natural and dry, pitted, cut.	1 cup	178	22	490	4	1	130	105	5.3	90	.16	.17	0
	Figs:													
240	Raw, small, 1½-inch diameter, about 12 per pound.	3 figs	114	78	90	1	Trace	23	40	.7	90	.07	.06	2
241	Dried, large, 2 by 1 inch	1 fig	21	23	60	1	Trace	15	26	.6	20	.02	.02	0
242	Fruit cocktail, canned in heavy sirup, solids and liquid.	1 cup	256	80	195	1	1	50	23	1.0	360	.04	.03	5
	Grapefruit:													
	Raw, medium, 4¼-inch diameter, size 64:													
243	White [4]	½ grapefruit	285	89	55	1	Trace	14	22	.6	10	.05	.02	52
244	Pink or red [4]	½ grapefruit	285	89	60	1	Trace	15	23	.6	640	.05	.02	52
245	Raw sections, white	1 cup	194	89	75	1	Trace	20	31	.8	20	.07	.03	72
	Canned, white:													
246	Sirup pack, solids and liquid.	1 cup	249	81	175	1	Trace	44	32	.7	20	.07	.04	75
247	Water pack, solids and liquid.	1 cup	240	91	70	1	Trace	18	31	.7	20	.07	.04	72
	Grapefruit juice:													
248	Fresh	1 cup	246	90	95	1	Trace	23	22	.5	(9)	.09	.04	92
	Canned, white:													
249	Unsweetened	1 cup	247	89	100	1	Trace	24	20	1.0	20	.07	.04	84
250	Sweetened	1 cup	250	86	130	1	Trace	32	20	1.0	20	.07	.04	78

	Frozen, concentrate, unsweetened:													
251	Undiluted, can, 6 fluid ounces.	1 can	207	62	300	4	1	72	70	.8	60	.29	.12	286
252	Diluted with 3 parts water, by volume.	1 cup	247	89	100	1	Trace	24	25	.2	20	.10	.04	96
	Frozen, concentrate, sweetened:													
253	Undiluted, can, 6 fluid ounces.	1 can	211	57	350	3	1	85	59	.6	50	.24	.11	245
254	Diluted with 3 parts water, by volume.	1 cup	249	88	115	1	Trace	28	20	.2	20	.08	.03	82
	Dehydrated:													
255	Crystals, can, net weight 4 ounces.	1 can	114	1	430	5	1	103	99	1.1	90	.41	.18	399
256	Prepared with water (1 pound yields about 1 gallon).	1 cup	247	90	100	1	Trace	24	22	.2	20	.10	.05	92
	Grapes, raw:													
257	American type (slip skin), such as Concord, Delaware, Niagara, Catawba, and Scuppernong.[4]	1 cup	153	82	65	1	1	15	15	.4	100	.05	.03	3
258	European type (adherent skin), such as Malaga, Muscat, Thompson Seedless, Emperor, and Flame Tokay.[4]	1 cup	160	81	95	1	Trace	25	17	.6	140	.07	.04	6
259	Grape juice, bottled or canned.	1 cup	254	83	165	1	Trace	42	28	.8	------	.10	.05	Trace
260	Lemons, raw, medium, 2⅕-inch diameter, size 150.[4]	1 lemon	106	90	20	1	Trace	6	18	.4	10	.03	.01	38
	Lemon juice:													
261	Fresh	1 cup	246	91	60	1	Trace	20	17	.5	40	.08	.03	113
262		1 tablespoon	15	91	5	Trace	Trace	1	1	Trace	Trace	Trace	Trace	7
263	Canned, unsweetened	1 cup	245	92	55	1	Trace	19	17	.5	40	.07	.03	102
	Lemonade concentrate, frozen, sweetened:													
264	Undiluted, can, 6 fluid ounces.	1 can	220	48	430	Trace	Trace	112	9	.4	40	.05	.06	66
265	Diluted with 4⅓ parts water, by volume.	1 cup	248	88	110	Trace	Trace	28	2	.1	10	.01	.01	17

[4] Measure and weight apply to entire vegetable or fruit including parts not usually eaten.

[8] About 5 milligrams per 8 fluid ounces is from cranberries. Ascorbic acid is usually added to approximately 100 milligrams per 8 fluid ounces.

[9] For white-fleshed varieties value is about 20 I.U. per cup; for red-fleshed varieties, 1,080 I.U. per cup.

No.	Food, approximate measure, and weight (in grams)	Measure	Weight	Water	Food energy	Protein	Fat (total lipid)	Carbohydrate	Calcium	Iron	Vitamin A value	Thiamine	Riboflavin	Ascorbic acid
	FRUITS AND FRUIT PRODUCTS—Con.													
	Lime juice:		*Grams*	*Percent*	*Calories*	*Grams*	*Grams*	*Grams*	*Milligrams*	*Milligrams*	*International units*	*Milligrams*	*Milligrams*	*Milligrams*
266	Fresh	1 cup	246	90	65	1	Trace	22	22	0.5	30	0.05	0.03	80
267	Canned	1 cup	246	90	65	1	Trace	22	22	.5	30	.05	.03	52
	Limeade concentrate, frozen, sweetened:													
268	Undiluted, can, 6 fluid ounces.	1 can	218	50	410	Trace	Trace	108	11	.2	Trace	.02	.02	26
269	Diluted with 4⅓ parts water, by volume.	1 cup	248	90	105	Trace	Trace	27	2	Trace	Trace	Trace	Trace	6
	Oranges, raw:													
270	California, Navel (winter), 2⅘-inch diameter, size 88.[4]	1 orange	180	85	60	2	Trace	16	49	.5	240	.12	.05	75
271	Florida, all varieties, 3-inch diameter.[4]	1 orange	210	86	75	1	Trace	19	67	.3	310	.16	.06	70
	Orange juice:													
	Fresh:													
272	California, Valencia (summer).	1 cup	249	88	115	2	1	26	27	.7	500	.22	.06	122
	Florida varieties:													
273	Early and midseason.	1 cup	247	90	100	1	Trace	23	25	.5	490	.22	.06	127
274	Late season, Valencia.	1 cup	248	88	110	1	Trace	26	25	.5	500	.22	.06	92
275	Canned, unsweetened	1 cup	249	87	120	2	Trace	28	25	1.0	500	.17	.05	100
	Frozen concentrate:													
276	Undiluted, can, 6 fluid ounces.	1 can	210	58	330	5	Trace	80	69	.8	1,490	.63	.10	332
277	Diluted with 3 parts water, by volume.	1 cup	248	88	110	2	Trace	27	22	.2	500	.21	.03	112
	Dehydrated:													
278	Crystals, can, net weight 4 ounces.	1 can	113	1	430	6	2	100	95	1.9	1,900	.76	.24	406

279	Prepared with water, 1 pound yields about 1 gallon.	1 cup	248	88	115	1	Trace	27	25	.5	500	.20	.06	108
	Orange and grapefruit juice:													
	Frozen concentrate:													
280	Undiluted, can, 6 fluid ounces.	1 can	209	59	325	4	1	78	61	.8	790	.47	.06	301
281	Diluted with 3 parts water, by volume.	1 cup	248	88	110	1	Trace	26	20	.2	270	.16	.02	102
282	Papayas, raw, ½-inch cubes.	1 cup	182	89	70	1	Trace	18	36	.5	3, 190	.07	.08	102
	Peaches:													
	Raw:													
283	Whole, medium, 2-inch diameter, about 4 per pound.[4]	1 peach	114	89	35	1	Trace	10	9	.5	[10]1,320	.02	.05	7
284	Sliced	1 cup	168	89	65	1	Trace	16	15	.8	[10]2,230	.03	.08	12
	Canned, yellow-fleshed, solids and liquid:													
	Sirup pack, heavy:													
285	Halves or slices	1 cup	257	79	200	1	Trace	52	10	.8	1, 100	.02	.06	7
286	Halves (medium) and sirup.	2 halves and 2 table-spoons sirup.	117	79	90	Trace	Trace	24	5	.4	500	.01	.03	3
287	Water pack	1 cup	245	91	75	1	Trace	20	10	.7	1, 100	.02	.06	7
288	Strained or chopped (baby food).	1 ounce	28	78	25	Trace	Trace	6	2	.1	140	Trace	.01	1
	Dried:													
289	Uncooked	1 cup	160	25	420	5	1	109	77	9.6	6, 240	.02	.31	28
290	Cooked, unsweet-ened, 10–12 halves and 6 tablespoons liquid.	1 cup	270	77	220	3	1	58	41	5.1	3, 290	.01	.15	6
	Frozen:													
291	Carton, 12 ounces, not thawed.	1 carton	340	76	300	1	Trace	77	14	1.7	2, 210	.03	.14	[11] 135
292	Can, 16 ounces, not thawed.	1 can	454	76	400	2	Trace	103	18	2.3	2, 950	.05	.18	[11] 181
293	Peach nectar, canned	1 cup	250	87	120	Trace	Trace	31	10	.5	1, 080	.02	.05	1
	Pears:													
294	Raw, 3 by 2½-inch diameter.[4]	1 pear	182	83	100	1	1	25	13	.5	30	.04	.07	7

[4] Measure and weight apply to entire vegetable or fruit including parts not usually eaten.

[10] Based on yellow-fleshed varieties; for white-fleshed varieties value is about 50 I.U. per 114-gram peach and 80 I.U. per cup of sliced peaches.

[11] Average weighted in accordance with commercial freezing practices. For products without added ascorbic acid, value is about 37 milligrams per 12-ounce carton and 50 milligrams per 16-ounce can; for those with added ascorbic acid, 139 milligrams per 12 ounces and 186 milligrams per 16 ounces.

No.	Food, approximate measure, and weight (in grams)			Water	Food energy	Protein	Fat (total lipid)	Carbohydrate	Calcium	Iron	Vitamin A value	Thiamine	Riboflavin	Ascorbic acid
	FRUITS AND FRUIT PRODUCTS—Con.													
	Pears—Continued													
	Canned, solids and liquid:													
	Sirup pack, heavy:		*Grams*	*Percent*	*Calories*	*Grams*	*Grams*	*Grams*	*Milligrams*	*Milligrams*	*International units*	*Milligrams*	*Milligrams*	*Milligrams*
295	Halves or slices	1 cup	255	80	195	1	1	50	13	0.5	Trace	0.03	0.05	4
296	Halves (medium) and sirup.	2 halves and 2 tablespoons sirup.	117	80	90	Trace	Trace	23	6	.2	Trace	.01	.02	2
297	Water pack	1 cup	243	91	80	Trace	Trace	20	12	.5	Trace	.02	.05	4
298	Strained or chopped (baby food).	1 ounce	28	82	20	Trace	Trace	5	2	.1	10	Trace	.01	1
299	Pear nectar, canned	1 cup	250	86	130	1	Trace	33	8	.2	Trace	.01	.05	1
300	Persimmons, Japanese or kaki, raw, seedless, 2½-inch diameter.[4]	1 persimmon	125	79	75	1	Trace	20	6	.4	2,740	.03	.02	11
	Pineapple:													
301	Raw, diced	1 cup	140	85	75	1	Trace	19	24	.7	100	.12	.04	24
	Canned, heavy sirup pack, solids and liquid:													
302	Crushed	1 cup	260	80	195	1	Trace	50	29	.8	120	.20	.06	17
303	Sliced, slices and juice.	2 small or 1 large and 2 tablespoons juice.	122	80	90	Trace	Trace	24	13	.4	50	.09	.03	8
304	Pineapple juice, canned	1 cup	249	86	135	1	Trace	34	37	.7	120	.12	.04	22
	Plums, all except prunes:													
305	Raw, 2-inch diameter, about 2 ounces.[4]	1 plum	60	87	25	Trace	Trace	7	7	.3	140	.02	.02	3
	Canned, sirup pack (Italian prunes):													
306	Plums (with pits) and juice.[4]	1 cup	256	77	205	1	Trace	53	22	2.2	2,970	.05	.05	4

307	Plums (without pits) and juice.	3 plums and 2 tablespoons juice.	122	77	100	Trace	Trace	26	11	1.1	1,470	.03	.02	2
	Prunes, dried, "softenized", medium:													
308	Uncooked [4]	4 prunes	32	28	70	1	Trace	18	14	1.1	440	.02	.04	1
309	Cooked, unsweetened, 17–18 prunes and ⅓ cup liquid.[4]	1 cup	270	66	295	2	1	78	60	4.5	1,860	.08	.18	2
310	Prunes with tapioca, canned, strained or junior (baby food).	1 ounce	28	77	25	Trace	Trace	6	2	.3	110	.01	.02	1
311	Prune juice, canned	1 cup	256	80	200	1	Trace	49	36	10.5	-------	.02	.03	4
312	Raisins, dried	1 cup	160	18	460	4	Trace	124	99	5.6	30	.18	.13	2
	Raspberries, red:													
313	Raw	1 cup	123	84	70	1	1	17	27	1.1	160	.04	.11	31
314	Frozen, 10-ounce carton, not thawed.	1 carton	284	74	275	2	1	70	37	1.7	200	.06	.17	59
315	Rhubarb, cooked, sugar added.	1 cup	272	63	385	1	Trace	98	212	1.6	220	.06	.15	17
	Strawberries:													
316	Raw, capped	1 cup	149	90	55	1	1	13	31	1.5	90	.04	.10	88
317	Frozen, 10-ounce carton, not thawed.	1 carton	284	71	310	1	1	79	40	2.0	90	.06	.17	150
318	Frozen, 16-ounce can, not thawed.	1 can	454	71	495	2	1	126	64	3.2	150	.09	.27	240
319	Tangerines, raw, medium, 2½-inch diameter, about 4 per pound.[4]	1 tangerine	114	87	40	1	Trace	10	34	.3	350	.05	.02	26
	Tangerine juice:													
320	Canned, unsweetened	1 cup	248	89	105	1	Trace	25	45	.5	1,040	.14	.04	56
	Frozen concentrate:													
321	Undiluted, can, 6 fluid ounces.	1 can	210	58	340	4	1	80	130	1.5	3,070	.43	.12	202
322	Diluted with 3 parts water, by volume.	1 cup	248	88	115	1	Trace	27	45	.5	1,020	.14	.04	67
323	Watermelon, raw, wedge, 4 by 8 inches (1/16 of 10 by 16-inch melon, about 2 pounds with rind).[4]	1 wedge	925	93	115	2	1	27	30	2.1	2,510	.13	.13	30

[4] Measure and weight apply to entire vegetable or fruit including parts not usually eaten.

No.	Food, approximate measure, and weight (in grams)			Water	Food energy	Protein	Fat (total lipid)	Carbohydrate	Calcium	Iron	Vitamin A value	Thiamine	Riboflavin	Ascorbic acid
			Grams	*Percent*	*Calories*	*Grams*	*Grams*	*Grams*	*Milligrams*	*Milligrams*	*International units*	*Milligrams*	*Milligrams*	*Milligrams*
	GRAIN PRODUCTS													
324	Barley, pearled, light, uncooked.	1 cup	203	11	710	17	2	160	32	4.1	0	0.25	0.17	0
325	Biscuits, baking powder with enriched flour, 2½-inch diameter.	1 biscuit	38	27	140	3	6	17	46	.6	Trace	.08	.08	Trace
326	Bran flakes (40 percent bran) added thiamine.	1 ounce	28	3	85	3	1	23	20	1.2	0	.11	.05	0
	Breads:													
327	Boston brown bread, slice, 3 by ¾ inch.	1 slice	48	45	100	3	1	22	43	.9	0	.05	.03	0
	Cracked-wheat bread:													
328	Loaf, 1-pound, 20 slices.	1 loaf	454	35	1,190	39	10	236	399	5.0	Trace	.53	.42	Trace
329	Slice	1 slice	23	35	60	2	1	12	20	.3	Trace	.03	.02	Trace
	French or vienna bread:													
330	Enriched, 1-pound loaf.	1 loaf	454	31	1,315	41	14	251	195	10.0	Trace	1.26	.98	Trace
331	Unenriched, 1-pound loaf.	1 loaf	454	31	1,315	41	14	251	195	3.2	Trace	.39	.39	Trace
	Italian bread:													
332	Enriched, 1-pound loaf.	1 loaf	454	32	1,250	41	4	256	77	10.0	0	1.31	.93	0
333	Unenriched, 1-pound loaf.	1 loaf	454	32	1,250	41	4	256	77	3.2	0	.39	.27	0
	Raisin bread:													
334	Loaf, 1-pound, 20 slices.	1 loaf	454	35	1,190	30	13	243	322	5.9	Trace	.24	.42	Trace
335	Slice	1 slice	23	35	60	2	1	12	16	.3	Trace	.01	.02	Trace
	Rye bread:													
	American, light (1/3 rye, 2/3 wheat):													
336	Loaf, 1-pound, 20 slices.	1 loaf	454	36	1,100	41	5	236	340	7.3	0	.81	.33	0
337	Slice	1 slice	23	36	55	2	Trace	12	17	.4	0	.04	.02	0

338	Pumpernickel, loaf, 1 pound.	1 loaf	454	34	1, 115	41	5	241	381	10. 9	0	1. 05	. 63	0
	White bread, enriched:													
	1 to 2 percent nonfat dry milk:													
339	Loaf, 1-pound, 20 slices.	1 loaf	454	36	1, 225	39	15	229	318	10. 9	Trace	1. 13	. 77	Trace
340	Slice	1 slice	23	36	60	2	1	12	16	. 6	Trace	. 06	. 04	Trace
	3 to 4 percent nonfat dry milk:[12]													
341	Loaf, 1-pound	1 loaf	454	36	1, 225	39	15	229	381	11. 3	Trace	1. 13	. 95	Trace
342	Slice, 20 per loaf	1 slice	23	36	60	2	1	12	19	. 6	Trace	. 06	. 05	Trace
343	Slice, toasted	1 slice	20	25	60	2	1	12	19	. 6	Trace	. 05	. 05	Trace
344	Slice, 26 per loaf	1 slice	17	36	45	1	1	9	14	. 4	Trace	. 04	. 04	Trace
	5 to 6 percent nonfat dry milk:													
345	Loaf, 1-pound, 20 slices.	1 loaf	454	35	1, 245	41	17	228	435	11. 3	Trace	1. 22	. 91	Trace
346	Slice	1 slice	23	35	65	2	1	12	22	. 6	Trace	. 06	. 05	Trace
	White bread, unenriched:													
	1 to 2 percent nonfat dry milk:													
347	Loaf, 1-pound, 20 slices.	1 loaf	454	36	1, 225	39	15	229	318	3. 2	Trace	. 40	. 36	Trace
348	Slice	1 slice	23	36	60	2	1	12	16	. 2	Trace	. 02	. 02	Trace
	3 to 4 percent nonfat dry milk:[12]													
349	Loaf, 1-pound	1 loaf	454	36	1, 225	39	15	229	381	3. 2	Trace	. 31	. 39	Trace
350	Slice, 20 per loaf	1 slice	23	36	60	2	1	12	19	. 2	Trace	. 02	. 02	Trace
351	Slice, toasted	1 slice	20	25	60	2	1	12	19	. 2	Trace	. 01	. 02	Trace
352	Slice, 26 per loaf	1 slice	17	36	45	1	1	9	14	. 1	Trace	. 01	. 01	Trace
	5 to 6 percent nonfat dry milk:													
353	Loaf, 1 pound, 20 slices.	1 loaf	454	35	1, 245	41	17	228	435	3. 2	Trace	. 32	. 59	Trace
354	Slice	1 slice	23	35	65	2	1	12	22	. 2	Trace	. 02	. 03	Trace
	Whole-wheat bread, made with 2 percent nonfat dry milk:													
355	Loaf, 1-pound, 20 slices	1 loaf	454	36	1, 105	48	14	216	449	10. 4	Trace	1. 17	. 56	Trace
356	Slice	1 slice	23	36	55	2	1	11	23	. 5	Trace	. 06	. 03	Trace
357	Slice, toasted	1 slice	19	24	55	2	1	11	22	. 5	Trace	. 05	. 03	Trace
358	Breadcrumbs, dry, grated	1 cup	88	6	345	11	4	65	107	3. 2	Trace	. 19	. 26	Trace
	Cakes:[13]													
359	Angelfood cake; sector, 2-inch (1/12 of 8-inch-diameter cake).	1 sector	40	32	110	3	Trace	24	4	. 1	0	Trace	. 06	0

[12] When the amount of nonfat dry milk in commercial white bread is unknown, values for bread with 3 to 4 percent nonfat dry milk are suggested.

[13] Unenriched cake flour and vegetable cooking fat used unless otherwise specified.

	Food, approximate measure, and weight (in grams)			Water	Food energy	Protein	Fat (total lipid)	Carbohydrate	Calcium	Iron	Vitamin A value	Thiamine	Riboflavin	Ascorbic acid
	GRAIN PRODUCTS—Continued													
	Cakes [13]—Continued		*Grams*	*Per-cent*	*Calo-ries*	*Grams*	*Grams*	*Grams*	*Milli-grams*	*Milli-grams*	*Inter-national units*	*Milli-grams*	*Milli-grams*	*Milli-grams*
360	Chocolate cake, chocolate icing; sector, 2-inch (1/16 of 10-inch-diameter layer cake).	1 sector	120	22	445	5	20	67	84	1.2	[14] 190	0.03	0.12	Trace
361	Fruitcake, dark (made with enriched flour); piece, 2 by 2 by 1/2 inch.	1 piece	30	18	115	1	5	18	22	.8	[14] 40	.04	.04	Trace
362	Gingerbread (made with enriched flour); piece, 2 by 2 by 2 inches.	1 piece	55	31	175	2	6	29	37	1.3	50	.06	.06	0
	Plain cake and cupcakes, without icing:													
363	Piece, 3 by 2 by 1 1/2 inches.	1 piece	55	24	200	2	8	31	35	.2	[14] 90	.01	.05	Trace
364	Cupcake, 2 3/4-inch diameter.	1 cupcake	40	24	145	2	6	22	26	.2	[14] 70	.01	.03	Trace
	Plain cake and cupcakes, with chocolate icing:													
365	Sector, 2-inch (1/16 of 10-inch-layer cake).	1 sector	100	21	370	4	14	59	63	.6	[14] 180	.02	.09	Trace
366	Cupcake, 2 3/4-inch diameter.	1 cupcake	50	21	185	2	7	30	32	.3	[14] 90	.01	.04	Trace
367	Poundcake, old-fashioned (equal weights flour, sugar, fat, eggs); slice, 2 3/4 by 3 by 5/8 inch.	1 slice	30	17	140	2	9	14	6	.2	[14] 80	.01	.03	0
368	Sponge cake; sector, 2-inch (1/12 of 8-inch-diameter cake).	1 sector	40	32	120	3	2	22	12	.5	180	.02	.06	Trace
	Cookies:													
369	Plain and assorted, 3-inch diameter.	1 cooky	25	3	120	1	5	18	9	.2	20	.01	.01	Trace

370	Fig bars, small	1 fig bar	16	14	55	1	1	12	12	.2	20	.01	.01	Trace
371	Corn, rice and wheat flakes, mixed, added nutrients.	1 ounce	28	3	110	2	Trace	24	11	.5	0	.11	------	0
	Corn flakes, added nutrients:													
372	Plain	1 ounce	28	4	110	2	Trace	24	5	.4	0	.12	.02	0
373	Sugar-covered	1 ounce	28	2	110	1	Trace	26	3	.3	0	.12	.01	0
	Corn grits, degermed, cooked:													
374	Enriched	1 cup	242	87	120	3	Trace	27	2	[15] .7	[16] 150	[15] .10	[15] .07	0
375	Unenriched	1 cup	242	87	120	3	Trace	27	2	.2	[16] 150	.05	.02	0
	Cornmeal, white or yellow, dry:													
376	Whole ground, unbolted	1 cup	118	12	420	11	5	87	24	2.8	[16] 600	.45	.13	0
377	Degermed, enriched	1 cup	145	12	525	11	2	114	9	[15] 4.2	[16] 640	[15] .64	[15] .38	0
378	Corn muffins, made with enriched degermed cornmeal and enriched flour; muffin, 2¾-inch diameter.	1 muffin	48	33	150	3	5	23	50	.8	[17] 80	.09	.11	Trace
379	Corn, puffed, presweetened, added nutrients.	1 ounce	28	5	110	1	Trace	26	3	.5	0	.12	.05	0
380	Corn, shredded, added nutrients.	1 ounce	28	3	110	2	Trace	25	1	.7	0	.12	.05	0
	Crackers:													
381	Graham, plain	4 small or 2 medium.	14	6	55	1	1	10	6	.2	0	.01	.03	0
382	Saltines, 2 inches square.	2 crackers	8	4	35	1	1	6	2	.1	0	Trace	Trace	0
	Soda:													
383	Cracker, 2½ inches square.	2 crackers	11	4	50	1	1	8	2	.2	0	Trace	Trace	0
384	Oyster crackers	10 crackers	10	4	45	1	1	7	2	.2	0	Trace	Trace	0
385	Cracker meal	1 tablespoon	10	6	45	1	1	7	2	.1	0	.01	Trace	0
386	Doughnuts, cake type	1 doughnut	32	24	125	1	6	16	13	[18] .4	30	[18] .05	[18] .05	Trace
387	Farina, regular, enriched, cooked.	1 cup	238	90	100	3	Trace	21	10	[15] .7	0	[15] .11	[15] .07	0

[13] Unenriched cake flour and vegetable cooking fat used unless otherwise specified.

[14] If the fat used in the recipe is butter or fortified margarine, the vitamin A value for chocolate cake with chocolate icing will be 490 I.U. per 2-inch sector, item 360; 100 I.U. for fruitcake, item 361; for plain cake without icing, 300 I.U. per piece, item 363; 220 I.U. per cupcake, item 364; for plain cake with icing, 440 I.U. per 2-inch sector, item 365; 220 I.U. per cupcake, item 366; and 300 I.U. for poundcake, item 367.

[15] Iron, thiamine, and riboflavin are based on the minimum levels of enrichment specified in standards of identity promulgated under the Federal Food, Drug, and Cosmetic Act.

[16] Vitamin A value based on yellow product. White product contains only a trace.

[17] Based on recipe using white cornmeal; if yellow is used, the vitamin A value is 140 I.U. per muffin.

[18] Based on product made with enriched flour. With unenriched flour, approximate values per doughnut are: Iron, 0.2 milligram; thiamine, 0.01 milligram; riboflavin, 0.03 milligram.

No.	Food, approximate measure, and weight (in grams)	Measure	Weight	Water	Food energy	Protein	Fat (total lipid)	Carbohydrate	Calcium	Iron	Vitamin A value	Thiamine	Riboflavin	Ascorbic acid
			Grams	*Percent*	*Calories*	*Grams*	*Grams*	*Grams*	*Milligrams*	*Milligrams*	*International units*	*Milligrams*	*Milligrams*	*Milligrams*
	GRAIN PRODUCTS—Continued													
	Macaroni, cooked:													
	Enriched:													
388	Cooked, firm stage (8 to 10 minutes; undergoes additional cooking in a food mixture).	1 cup	130	64	190	6	1	39	14	[15] 1.4	0	[15] 0.23	[15] 0.14	0
389	Cooked until tender	1 cup	140	72	155	5	1	32	11	[15] 1.3	0	[15] .19	[15] .11	0
	Unenriched:													
390	Cooked, firm stage (8 to 10 minutes; undergoes additional cooking in a food mixture).	1 cup	130	64	190	6	1	39	14	.6	0	.02	.02	0
391	Cooked until tender	1 cup	140	72	155	5	1	32	11	.6	0	.02	.02	0
392	Macaroni (enriched) and cheese, baked.	1 cup	220	58	470	18	24	44	398	2.0	950	.22	.44	Trace
393	Muffins, with enriched white flour; muffin, 2¾-inch diameter.	1 muffin	48	38	140	4	5	20	50	.8	50	.08	.11	Trace
	Noodles (egg noodles), cooked:													
394	Enriched	1 cup	160	70	200	7	2	37	16	[15] 1.4	110	[15] .23	[15] .14	0
395	Unenriched	1 cup	160	70	200	7	2	37	16	1.0	110	.04	.03	0
396	Oats (with or without corn) puffed, added nutrients.	1 ounce	28	3	115	3	2	21	50	1.3	0	.28	.05	0
397	Oatmeal or rolled oats, regular or quick-cooking, cooked.	1 cup	236	86	130	5	2	23	21	1.4	0	.19	.05	0
	Pancakes (griddlecakes), 4-inch diameter:													
398	Wheat, enriched flour (home recipe).	1 cake	27	50	60	2	2	9	27	.4	30	.05	.06	Trace

399	Buckwheat (buckwheat pancake mix, made with egg and milk).	1 cake	27	58	55	2	2	6	59	.4	60	.03	.04	Trace
	Piecrust, plain, baked:													
	Enriched flour:													
400	Lower crust, 9-inch shell.	1 crust	135	15	675	8	45	59	19	2.3	0	.27	.19	0
401	Double crust, 9-inch pie.	1 double crust	270	15	1,350	16	90	118	38	4.6	0	.55	.39	0
	Unenriched flour:													
402	Lower crust, 9-inch shell.	1 crust	135	15	675	8	45	59	19	.7	0	.04	.04	0
403	Double crust, 9-inch pie.	1 double crust	270	15	1,350	16	90	118	38	1.4	0	.08	.07	0
	Pies (piecrust made with unenriched flour); sector, 4-inch, 1/7 of 9-inch-diameter pie:													
404	Apple	1 sector	135	48	345	3	15	51	11	.4	40	.03	.02	1
405	Cherry	1 sector	135	47	355	4	15	52	19	.4	590	.03	.03	1
406	Custard	1 sector	130	58	280	8	14	30	125	.8	300	.07	.21	0
407	Lemon meringue	1 sector	120	47	305	4	12	45	17	.6	200	.04	.10	4
408	Mince	1 sector	135	43	365	3	16	56	38	1.4	Trace	.09	.05	1
409	Pumpkin	1 sector	130	59	275	5	15	32	66	.6	3,210	.04	.13	Trace
410	Pizza (cheese); 5½-inch sector; ⅛ of 14-inch-diameter pie.	1 sector	75	45	185	7	6	27	107	.7	290	.04	.12	4
411	Popcorn, popped, with added oil and salt.	1 cup	14	3	65	1	3	8	1	.3	------	------	.01	0
412	Pretzels, small stick	5 sticks	5	8	20	Trace	Trace	4	1	0	0	Trace	Trace	0
	Rice, white (fully milled or polished), enriched, cooked:													
413	Common commercial varieties, all types.	1 cup	168	73	185	3	Trace	41	17	[19] 1.5	0	[19] .19	[19] .01	0
414	Long grain, parboiled	1 cup	176	73	185	4	Trace	41	33	[19] 1.4	0	[19] .19	[19] .02	0
415	Rice, puffed, added nutrients (without salt).	1 cup	14	4	55	1	Trace	13	3	.3	0	.06	.01	0

[15] Iron, thiamine, and riboflavin are based on the minimum levels of enrichment specified in standards of identity promulgated under the Federal Food, Drug, and Cosmetic Act.

[19] Iron and thiamine are based on the minimum levels of enrichment specified in standards of identity promulgated under the Federal Food, Drug, and Cosmetic Act. Riboflavin is based on unenriched rice. When the minimum level of enrichment for riboflavin specified in the standards of identity becomes effective the value will be 0.12 milligram per cup of parboiled rice and of white rice.

No.	Food, approximate measure, and weight (in grams)			Water	Food energy	Protein	Fat (total lipid)	Carbohydrate	Calcium	Iron	Vitamin A value	Thiamine	Riboflavin	Ascorbic acid
	GRAIN PRODUCTS—Continued		*Grams*	*Percent*	*Calories*	*Grams*	*Grams*	*Grams*	*Milligrams*	*Milligrams*	*International units*	*Milligrams*	*Milligrams*	*Milligrams*
416	Rice flakes, added nutrients.	1 cup	30	3	115	2	Trace	26	9	0.5	0	0.10	0.02	0
	Rolls:													
	Plain, pan; 12 per 16 ounces:													
417	Enriched	1 roll	38	31	115	3	2	20	28	.7	Trace	.11	.07	Trace
418	Unenriched	1 roll	38	31	115	3	2	20	28	.3	Trace	.02	.03	Trace
419	Hard, round; 12 per 22 ounces.	1 roll	52	25	160	5	2	31	24	.4	Trace	.03	.05	Trace
420	Sweet, pan; 12 per 18 ounces.	1 roll	43	32	135	4	4	21	37	.3	30	.03	.06	Trace
421	Rye wafers, whole-grain, 1⅞ by 3½ inches.	2 wafers	13	6	45	2	Trace	10	7	.5	0	.04	.03	0
	Spaghetti:													
	Cooked, tender stage (14 to 20 minutes):													
422	Enriched	1 cup	140	72	155	5	1	32	11	[15] 1.3	0	[15] .19	[15] .11	0
423	Unenriched	1 cup	140	72	155	5	1	32	11	.6	0	.02	.02	0
424	Spaghetti with meat balls in tomato sauce (home recipe).	1 cup	250	70	335	19	12	39	125	3.8	1,600	.26	.30	22
425	Spaghetti in tomato sauce with cheese (home recipe).	1 cup	250	77	260	9	9	37	80	2.2	1,080	.24	.18	14
426	Waffles, with enriched flour, ½ by 4½ by 5½ inches.	1 waffle	75	41	210	7	7	28	85	1.3	250	.13	.19	Trace
	Wheat, puffed:													
427	With added nutrients (without salt).	1 ounce	28	3	105	4	Trace	22	8	1.2	0	.15	.07	0
428	With added nutrients, with sugar and honey.	1 ounce	28	3	105	2	1	25	7	.9	0	.14	.05	0

429	Wheat, rolled; cooked	1 cup	236	80	175	5	1	40	19	1.7	0	.17	.06	0
430	Wheat, shredded, plain (long, round, or bite-size).	1 ounce	28	7	100	3	1	23	12	1.0	0	.06	.03	0
431	Wheat and malted barley flakes, with added nutrients.	1 ounce	28	3	110	2	Trace	24	14	.7	0	.13	.03	0
432	Wheat flakes, with added nutrients.	1 ounce	28	4	100	3	Trace	23	12	1.2	0	.18	.04	0
	Wheat flours:													
433	Whole-wheat, from hard wheats, stirred.	1 cup	120	12	400	16	2	85	49	4.0	0	.66	.14	0
	All-purpose or family flour:													
434	Enriched, sifted	1 cup	110	12	400	12	1	84	18	[15] 3.2	0	[15] .48	[15] .29	0
435	Unenriched, sifted	1 cup	110	12	400	12	1	84	18	.9	0	.07	.05	0
436	Self-rising, enriched	1 cup	110	11	385	10	1	82	292	[15] 3.2	0	[15] .49	[15] .29	0
437	Cake or pastry flour, sifted.	1 cup	100	12	365	8	1	79	17	.5	0	.03	.03	0
438	Wheat germ, crude, commercially milled.	1 cup	68	11	245	18	7	32	49	6.4	0	1.36	.46	0
	FATS, OILS													
	Butter, 4 sticks per pound:													
439	Sticks, 2	1 cup	227	16	1,625	1	184	1	45	0	[20] 7,500	------	------	0
440	Stick, ⅛	1 tablespoon	14	16	100	Trace	11	Trace	3	0	[20] 460	------	------	0
441	Pat or square (64 per pound).	1 pat	7	16	50	Trace	6	Trace	1	0	[20] 230	------	------	0
	Fats, cooking:													
442	Lard	1 cup	220	0	1,985	0	220	0	0	0	0	0	0	0
443	Lard	1 tablespoon	14	0	125	0	14	0	0	0	0	0	0	0
444	Vegetable fats	1 cup	200	0	1,770	0	200	0	0	0	------	0	0	0
445	Vegetable fats	1 tablespoon	12.5	0	110	0	12	0	0	0	------	0	0	0
	Margarine, 4 sticks per pound:													
446	Sticks, 2	1 cup	227	16	1,635	1	184	1	45	0	[21] 7,500	------	------	0
447	Stick, ⅛	1 tablespoon	14	16	100	Trace	11	Trace	3	0	[21] 460	------	------	0
448	Pat or square (64 per pound).	1 pat	7	16	50	Trace	6	Trace	1	0	[21] 230	------	------	0
	Oils, salad or cooking:													
449	Corn	1 tablespoon	14	0	125	0	14	0	0	0	------	0	0	0
450	Cottonseed	1 tablespoon	14	0	125	0	14	0	0	0	------	0	0	0
451	Olive	1 tablespoon	14	0	125	0	14	0	0	0	------	0	0	0
452	Soybean	1 tablespoon	14	0	125	0	14	0	0	0	------	0	0	0

[15] Iron, thiamine, and riboflavin are based on the minimum levels of enrichment specified in standards of identity promulgated under the Federal Food, Drug, and Cosmetic Act.

[20] Year-round average.

[21] Based on the average vitamin A content of fortified margarine. Federal specifications for fortified margarine require a minimum of 15,000 I.U. of vitamin A per pound.

No.	Food, approximate measure, and weight (in grams)			Water	Food energy	Protein	Fat (total lipid)	Carbohydrate	Calcium	Iron	Vitamin A value	Thiamine	Riboflavin	Ascorbic acid
	FATS, OILS—Continued													
			Grams	*Percent*	*Calories*	*Grams*	*Grams*	*Grams*	*Milligrams*	*Milligrams*	*International units*	*Milligrams*	*Milligrams*	*Milligrams*
	Salad dressings:													
453	Blue cheese	1 tablespoon	16	32	80	1	8	1	13	Trace	30	Trace	0.02	Trace
454	Commercial, mayonnaise type.	1 tablespoon	15	41	65	Trace	6	2	2	Trace	30	Trace	Trace	------
455	French	1 tablespoon	15	39	60	Trace	6	3	2	.1	------	------	------	------
456	Home cooked, boiled	1 tablespoon	17	68	30	1	2	3	15	.1	80	.01	.03	Trace
457	Mayonnaise	1 tablespoon	15	15	110	Trace	12	Trace	3	.1	40	Trace	.01	------
458	Thousand island	1 tablespoon	15	32	75	Trace	8	2	2	.1	50	Trace	Trace	Trace
	SUGARS, SWEETS													
	Candy:													
459	Caramels	1 ounce	28	8	115	1	3	22	42	.4	Trace	.01	.05	Trace
460	Chocolate, milk, plain	1 ounce	28	1	150	2	9	16	65	.3	80	.02	.09	Trace
461	Fudge, plain	1 ounce	28	8	115	1	3	21	22	.3	Trace	.01	.03	Trace
462	Hard candy	1 ounce	28	1	110	0	Trace	28	6	.5	0	0	0	0
463	Marshmallows	1 ounce	28	17	90	1	Trace	23	5	.5	0	0	Trace	0
464	Chocolate sirup, thin type	1 tablespoon	20	32	50	Trace	Trace	13	3	.3	------	Trace	.01	0
465	Honey, strained or extracted.	1 tablespoon	21	17	65	Trace	0	17	1	.1	0	Trace	.01	Trace
466	Jams and preserves	1 tablespoon	20	29	55	Trace	Trace	14	4	.2	Trace	Trace	.01	Trace
467	Jellies	1 tablespoon	20	29	55	Trace	Trace	14	4	.3	Trace	Trace	.01	1
	Molasses, cane:													
468	Light (first extraction)	1 tablespoon	20	24	50	------	------	13	33	.9	------	.01	.01	------
469	Blackstrap (third extraction).	1 tablespoon	20	24	45	------	------	11	137	3.2	------	.02	.04	------
470	Sirup, table blends (chiefly corn, light and dark).	1 tablespoon	20	24	60	0	0	15	9	.8	0	0	0	0
	Sugars (cane or beet):													
471	Granulated	1 cup	200	Trace	770	0	0	199	0	.2	0	0	0	0
472		1 tablespoon	12	Trace	45	0	0	12	0	Trace	0	0	0	0
473	Lump, 1⅛ by ¾ by ⅜	1 lump	6	Trace	25	0	0	6	0	Trace	0	0	0	0
474	Powdered, stirred before measuring.	1 cup	128	Trace	495	0	0	127	0	.1	0	0	0	0
475		1 tablespoon	8	Trace	30	0	0	8	0	Trace	0	0	0	0

476	Brown, firm-packed	1 cup	220	2	820	0	0	212	187	7.5	0	.02	.07	0
477		1 tablespoon	14	2	50	0	0	13	12	.5	0	Trace	Trace	0
	MISCELLANEOUS ITEMS													
478	Beer (average 3.6 percent alcohol by weight).	1 cup	240	92	100	1	0	9	12	Trace	----	.01	.07	----
	Beverages, carbonated:													
479	Cola type	1 cup	240	90	95	0	0	24	----	----	0	0	0	0
480	Ginger ale	1 cup	230	92	70	0	0	18	----	----	0	0	0	0
481	Bouillon cube, ⅝ inch	1 cube	4	4	5	1	Trace	Trace	----	----	----	----	----	----
	Chili powder. *See* Vegetables, peppers.													
482	Chili sauce (mainly tomatoes).	1 tablespoon	17	68	20	Trace	Trace	4	3	.1	240	.02	.01	3
	Chocolate:													
483	Bitter or baking	1 ounce	28	2	145	3	15	8	22	1.9	20	.01	.07	0
484	Sweet	1 ounce	28	1	150	1	10	16	27	.4	Trace	.01	.04	Trace
	Cider. *See* Fruits, apple juice.													
	Gelatin, dry:													
485	Plain	1 tablespoon	10	13	35	9	Trace	----	----	----	----	----	----	----
486	Dessert powder, 3-ounce package.	½ cup	85	2	315	8	0	75	----	----	----	----	----	----
	Gelatin dessert, ready-to-eat:													
487	Plain	1 cup	239	84	140	4	0	34	----	----	----	----	----	----
488	With fruit	1 cup	241	82	160	3	Trace	40	----	----	----	----	----	----
	Olives, pickled:													
489	Green	4 medium or 3 extra large or 2 giant.	16	78	15	Trace	2	Trace	8	.2	40	----	----	----
490	Ripe: Mission	3 small or 2 large.	10	73	15	Trace	2	Trace	9	.1	10	Trace	Trace	----
	Pickles, cucumber:													
491	Dill, large, 4 by 1¾ inches.	1 pickle	135	93	15	1	Trace	3	35	1.4	140	Trace	.03	8
492	Sweet, 2¾ by ¾ inches	1 pickle	20	61	30	Trace	Trace	7	2	.2	20	Trace	Trace	1
	Popcorn. *See* Grain products.													
493	Sherbet, orange	1 cup	193	67	260	2	2	59	31	Trace	110	.02	.06	4
	Soups, canned; ready-to-serve (prepared with equal volume of water):													
494	Bean with pork	1 cup	250	84	170	8	6	22	62	2.2	650	.14	.07	2
495	Beef noodle	1 cup	250	93	70	4	3	7	8	1.0	50	.05	.06	Trace
496	Beef bouillon, broth, consomme.	1 cup	240	96	30	5	0	3	Trace	.5	Trace	Trace	.02	----

	Food, approximate measure, and weight (in grams)			Water	Food energy	Protein	Fat (total lipid)	Carbohydrate	Calcium	Iron	Vitamin A value	Thiamine	Riboflavin	Ascorbic acid
	MISCELLANEOUS ITEMS—Continued													
	Soups, canned; ready-to-serve—Con.		*Grams*	*Percent*	*Calories*	*Grams*	*Grams*	*Grams*	*Milligrams*	*Milligrams*	*International units*	*Milligrams*	*Milligrams*	*Milligrams*
497	Chicken noodle	1 cup	250	93	65	4	2	8	10	0.5	50	0.02	0.02	Trace
498	Clam chowder	1 cup	255	92	85	2	3	13	36	1.0	920	.03	.03	------
499	Cream soup (mushroom)	1 cup	240	90	135	2	10	10	41	.5	70	.02	.12	Trace
500	Minestrone	1 cup	245	90	105	5	3	14	37	1.0	2,350	.07	.05	------
501	Pea, green	1 cup	245	86	130	6	2	23	44	1.0	340	.05	.05	7
502	Tomato	1 cup	245	90	90	2	2	16	15	.7	1,000	.06	.05	12
503	Vegetable with beef broth.	1 cup	250	92	80	3	2	14	20	.8	3,250	.05	.02	------
504	Starch (cornstarch)	1 cup	128	12	465	Trace	Trace	112	0	0	0	0	0	0
505		1 tablespoon	8	12	30	Trace	Trace	7	0	0	0	0	0	0
506	Tapioca, quick-cooking	1 cup	152	13	535	1	Trace	131	15	.6	0	0	0	0
507	granulated, dry, stirred before measuring.	1 tablespoon	10	13	35	Trace	Trace	9	1	Trace	0	0	0	0
508	Vinegar	1 tablespoon	15	------	2	0	------	1	1	.1	------	------	------	------
509	White sauce, medium	1 cup	265	73	430	10	33	23	305	.5	1,220	.12	.44	Trace
	Yeast:													
	Baker's:													
510	Compressed	1 ounce	28	71	25	3	Trace	3	4	1.4	Trace	.20	.47	Trace
511	Dry active	1 ounce	28	5	80	10	Trace	11	12	4.6	Trace	.66	1.53	Trace
512	Brewer's, dry, debittered.	1 tablespoon	8	5	25	3	Trace	3	17	1.4	Trace	1.25	.34	Trace
	Yoghurt. *See* Milk, cream, cheese; related products.													

Alcoholic Beverages

The number of calories in alcoholic beverages depends on the per cent of alcohol, usually expressed as *proof*, and the amount of sugar in the wines or mixes.

Whiskey, gin, rum—1½ ounces (1 jigger)
- 100 proof .... 125 calories
- 90 proof .... 110 calories
- 86 proof .... 105 calories
- 80 proof .... 100 calories
- 70 proof .... 85 calories

Wines—3 ounces—1 wine glass
- Table wines (such as Chablis, claret, Rhine wine, and sauterne) .... 75 calories
- Dessert wines (such as muscatel, port, sherry, and Tokay) .... 125 calories

Index